STUDY SKILLS FOR ADULTS RETURNING TO SCHOOL

STUDY SKILLS FOR ADULTS RETURNING TO SCHOOL

SECOND EDITION

Jerold W. Apps

Professor of Continuing Education
Department of Continuing and
Vocational Education
University of Wisconsin-Madison

McGRAW-HILL BOOK COMPANY
New York St. Louis San Francisco Auckland Bogotá
Hamburg Johannesburg London Madrid Mexico Montreal New Delhi
Panama Paris São Paulo Singapore Sydney Tokyo Toronto

This book was set in Times Roman by Bi-Comp, Incorporated.
The editors were Donald W. Burden and Edwin Hanson;
the cover was designed by Anne Canevari Green;
the production supervisor was Diane Renda.
R. R. Donnelley & Sons Company was printer and binder.

STUDY SKILLS FOR ADULTS RETURNING TO SCHOOL

2 3 4 5 6 7 8 9 0   DODO   8 9 8 7 6 5 4 3 2 1

Library of Congress Cataloging in Publication Data

Apps, Jerold W., date
    Study skills for adults returning to school.

    Previous ed. published in 1978 as: Study skills
for those adults returning to school.
    Includes index.
    1. Study, Method of. 2. Adult education.
I. Title.
LB1049.A66 1982   374'.02   81-3749
ISBN 0-07-002165-1   AACR2

374.02
ap652

CONTENTS

PREFACE

I have been gratified with the response to the first edition of this book. Adults returning to school across the country have told me they've found the book useful at a time when they had many questions and faced an array of problems concerning their return to formal study.

This revised edition is intended to provide an even more useful resource to the returning student. Besides bringing up to date various statistical information, I have incorporated several additional self-study exercises in this edition. Also, at the beginning of the book, I've included a "Self-Rating Chart" so returning students can do a self-assessment of their current study skills. Once this is done, the student can turn directly to the section of the book where that particular study skill is discussed.

Concentration and time management are two problems that plague many returning students. I have added both more information and several self-study exercises that focus on these areas.

Finally, because instructors of study skills courses and workshops are using this book as a resource, an instructor's guide has been prepared with suggestions on how to use this book in a course or workshop setting. The instructor's guides can be ordered directly from the McGraw-Hill Book Company.

I remember clearly when I returned to graduate school after working 10 years and taking courses on a part-time basis.

"Why don't you ask your parents for tuition money?" the counselor at the student loan office inquired.

For a moment I couldn't say a word, the question sounded so incredible.

I answered quietly, "My parents are retired and have a very limited income."

"Retired?" the counselor muttered, implying, "How could they do that to me?"

"Do you realize that I am 31 years old, that I am married and have three children—and that I need tuition money if I am going to spend a year in school?" I asked quietly.

"But why are you returning to school?" was all the counselor could reply.

I didn't fit any of the normal patterns, particularly for the loan counselor, who had a set of questions that fit the more traditional, younger student who was beginning graduate education immediately after completing an undergraduate program.

Not even the forms fit. I found that my grades were sent to my parents when I completed a semester of graduate work. Frankly, my wife was much more interested in how I was doing.

Besides, my parents had some problems understanding why I was going back to school again anyway. I had already gone back once before, when I returned from the Army. This somehow seemed appropriate to them then, for many veterans were returning to college. Some of my relatives couldn't understand it at all. "Got tired of working, huh?" an uncle said to me when he learned I was back in school and working on another degree.

All my relatives and friends felt sorry for my wife and children, with Daddy back in school. There was no small amount of guilt to deal with. Except for a very understanding wife and three tolerant children, I probably would have given it all up. I had demonstrated that I could make a living without doing additional graduate work, hadn't I?

During the past 17 years as a professor of continuing education, I have worked with many mature adults who returned to school; some for undergraduate degrees, some for graduate degrees, and some simply because they wanted to take some courses on a part-time basis and weren't concerned about acquiring a degree.

Many of the same feelings I experienced were communicated to me as we talked about their study programs. Some of the same problems I faced, these students faced. The returning student is no longer an oddity, but makes up a sizable proportion of the student population at many colleges and universities. According to the Census Bureau, in fall 1979 one in three college students was 25 or older. Of all college students enrolled in fall 1979, 33.6 percent of the men and 37.8 percent of the women were 25 and older. Most of these returning students were enrolled part time. About a sixth of the full-time students were at least 25 years of age.

I have worked with returning students who are in their late twenties, and I have worked with returning students in their fifties. All wonder if they will be able to do formal educational work after several years away. All wonder how they will relate to younger students. Most wonder if they will be the only older student in the classes they will take. (This concern can be quickly dealt with by referring to the statistics cited above).

In addition to counseling many returning students, I have had them in the courses I teach and I have worked with them on research projects I have directed.

Before becoming a professor of continuing education, I worked for several years as a practicing adult educator, working directly with adults of various ages. These years helped me to understand something about adults as learners: what interested them, what got in the way of their learning, the teaching approaches they preferred, and the relationships with the instructor that seemed to enhance learning. I also learned early in my career how much there was to be learned from students if I as "instructor" would be open to them and what they had to share.

I say all of this because I think you, as the reader of this book and one who has returned to school or is planning to do some formal course work, deserve to know something about my experience and background.

This book is designed for returning students who want to sharpen their study skills and who, in a broader sense, want to learn how to learn better. It is a practical book with an emphasis on solving problems that returning students face.

Materials for this book have been gathered from several sources. An informal questionnaire was given to two small groups of returning students at the University of Wisconsin-Madison, and at Northern Illinois University. Sixteen responses were received from these students about such issues as what problems they faced in returning to school; where they received help; how long it took "to become a student" again; and what kinds of information, guides, etc., would be helpful to them.

I drew heavily on my years of teaching and counseling experience with older students. I also drew from the expanding literature within the field of adult education on such topics as adult learning, helping people become autonomous learners, and planning learning for adults.

I reviewed a host of "how to study in college" books. Unfortunately all were slanted toward those students entering college directly from high school. I drew upon the McGraw-Hill Basic Skills System for ideas and several exercises that I believed would be of interest to adults returning to school.

For this revised edition I followed many of the suggestions offered by Ramona Knowls, San Francisco State University; Sister Joyce Klinger, College of St. Francis, Joliet, Illinois; and my editor, Donald Burden. And, finally, I particularly listened to returning students who told me what they wanted to see in the revised edition of the book.

The book begins with an exercise to rate your own study skills.

Chapter 1 gives you background information about the returning adult student. It attempts to answer such questions as: What are the characteristics of the returning student? How does the aging process affect learning? What blocks learning in adult students? How does one go about learning how to learn?

Chapter 2 focuses on how to take notes, how to listen better, and how to prepare for and take examinations.

Chapter 3 focuses on improving your reading ability. It stresses learning how to read at various levels, from reading in an overview for the main ideas to reading in order to create new ideas.

Chapter 4 provides specific information on how to improve your writing skills, particularly as they relate to writing term papers and reports.

Chapter 5 is concerned with how you can improve your thinking. It outlines two general approaches to thinking—rational, or problem-solving, thinking and creative thinking—and gives specific suggestions on how to do each.

Chapter 6 provides specific ideas on how you can increase your vocabulary within the context of the material you are reading.

In Chapter 7 the focus is on effectively using resources that are available in most colleges and universities, including the library, professors, the community, and helping centers.

Chapter 8 is written specifically for the student returning to a graduate school. It discusses the particular problems faced by graduate students, the planning of graduate programs, and the research requirement that is a part of many graduate programs.

Chapter 9 gives you some suggestions on how you and your fellow students can have a voice in continuing to improve a system that was originally designed for persons continuing their education from high school.

I am indebted to many people for the preparation of this book. I particularly want to mention Dr. Richard Johnson, associate director, Student Counseling Services, and Prudence Stewart, counselor, Educational Placement and Career Services (herself a returning student) for reviewing and critically commenting on the rough draft of the manuscript.

Dr. Donald Campbell, director, Office of Continuing Education for Health Professionals, University of Illinois College of Medicine, and Dr.

Chere Coggins, academic planner, the University of Wisconsin System, read several chapters and offered much critical comment.

Margaret Geisler, director, Continuing Education Services; Dr. Joseph Corry, assistant vice chancellor and director of continuing education programs; and Steve Saffian, director of the Campus Assistance Center, all at the University of Wisconsin-Madison, offered many useful suggestions for this book.

And I especially thank my wife Ruth, and daughter Susan, who spent many hours helping put the manuscript into final form.

Jerold W. Apps

RATE YOUR STUDY SKILLS

You will find this book most useful if you complete the self-rating chart before you begin reading. After completing the self-rating, put in priority order those items you checked "often a problem," followed by those checked "sometimes a problem." Then begin in the book on those pages that deal with that item. All returning students should read pages 1–14 of Chapter 1, which covers general concerns.

SELF-RATING CHART

Consider each of the items listed below. Check the extent to which the item is a problem for you. To the right of each item are page numbers where information on this topic is discussed in the book.

Priority		Not a problem	Sometimes a problem	Often a problem	Reference
_____	1 Attitude about learning ability	_____	_____	_____	pp. 7–11
_____	2 Time management	_____	_____	_____	pp. 12–17
_____	3 Ability to concentrate	_____	_____	_____	pp. 17–20
_____	4 Ability to plan own learning	_____	_____	_____	pp. 20–25

Priority		Not a problem	Sometimes a problem	Often a problem	Reference
———	5 Taking lecture notes	———	———	———	pp. 30–36
———	6 Listening	———	———	———	pp. 37–41
———	7 Examinations	———	———	———	pp. 41–49
———	8 Reading speed	———	———	———	pp. 53–56
———	9 Reading comprehension	———	———	———	pp. 56–61
———	10 Reading for different purposes	———	———	———	pp. 63–78
———	11 Overview reading	———	———	———	pp. 63–66
———	12 Marking reading material	———	———	———	pp. 57–58
———	13 Taking notes from reading	———	———	———	pp. 59–60
———	14 Writing understandable writing	———	———	———	pp. 82–89
———	15 Writing a major report	———	———	———	pp. 89–97
———	16 Evaluating own writing	———	———	———	pp. 96–98
———	17 Sexism in writing	———	———	———	pp. 97, 99–100
———	18 Preparing a manuscript	———	———	———	p. 101
———	19 Process of rational thinking	———	———	———	pp. 112–117
———	20 Process of creative thinking	———	———	———	pp. 117–123
———	21 Learning new words	———	———	———	pp. 129–142
———	22 Knowing study resources	———	———	———	pp. 144–148
———	23 Using libraries	———	———	———	pp. 148–157
———	24 Planning a graduate program	———	———	———	pp. 164–171

STUDY SKILLS FOR ADULTS RETURNING TO SCHOOL

LEARNING HOW TO LEARN

For many persons learning is something that is directed by others. You attend a class and accept that the teacher organizes the content, tells you what books to read, gives you assignments to complete, and tests you to give you a grade. In this example, the teacher directs your learning. Most persons view learning as something that is done in some organized fashion in schools where there are classes and courses and curricula that are preplanned and packaged and where students enroll with the hope of learning something from the experience.

The concept of learning how to learn challenges the attitude that others are responsible for planning your learning. The underlying assumption of learning how to learn is that you, the learner, have the ability and the responsibility for planning much of your own learning. That is not to say that at times you will not call on others for help. Indeed you will, particularly if you are beginning study in an area that is relatively or completely new to you. But even in new areas, most of you, with some guidelines, can make a major input into planning your learning.

Learning how to learn, then, can be defined as taking charge of your learning. It is a skill that will help you as you enroll in courses and classes, but it is also a skill that will assist you as you pursue lifelong learning.

Before discussing the process of learning how to learn, we must spend some time with several basic questions: What is learning? What are some of the blocks to learning? How can these blocks be overcome?

WHAT LEARNING IS

You would think that educators could very quickly define learning and, as a group, agree on the definition. Unfortunately this is not the case. In many ways it is a paradox. Educators are concerned about learning and helping people to learn, yet as a group they cannot agree on what it is.

Much research has been done and continues to be done on the question, What is learning? But no one yet has discovered what exactly goes on within a person during the process of learning. In fact educators cannot even agree on what are the outcomes of learning.

Learning theorists have grouped themselves into three camps: (1) behaviorists, represented today by B. F. Skinner; (2) cognitive field theorists, represented by writers such as Jerome J. Bruner and David Ausubel; and (3) humanists, represented by such persons as Carl Rogers, Abraham Maslow, and Fritz Perls.

Depending on which of these camps educators subscribe to, their definition of learning comes out somewhat differently and the process by which learning best occurs varies as well.

For our purposes we will describe learning as follows.

Learning Is Doing

It is an active process in which you must be involved. You do not learn effectively by sitting on the sidelines; you must be involved and participating in what it is you are trying to learn.

Learning Is Changing

Though there is considerable controversy among educators concerning a definition of learning, they all appear to agree on one point: When someone has learned, he or she has changed. Learners are different after they have participated in learning compared with before they began. Perhaps this seems self-evident in many ways. If you have learned how to type, obviously you have changed. You know something about the history of your state after taking a course in it. You are different from the way you were before enrolling in that course, if only in that you now have information that you didn't previously have.

If in a weekend workshop you examined some of your attitudes about minority groups and found yourself wanting to do further examination, you have changed. You are now a different person compared with before you enrolled in the workshop.

Learning Can Be Planned or Incidental

You can participate in a formal course designed to help you learn how to fill out income tax forms. You can view a series of TV programs on social problems in your community and then participate with some of your neighbors in a group discussion about these issues. You can enroll in a correspondence course to improve your writing. In all these examples, the learning is planned. You are enrolling in the course, watching the television programs, and participating in the correspondence course with the specific intent of learning something.

Often overlooked is the learning that is not planned, which we call *incidental learning*. All of us can recall learning many useful things in our various jobs without intending to do so. It is impossible to live a day without learning something.

Incidental learning usually occurs when we are involved in planned learning. We learn things in addition to what has been planned.

Unfortunately our society has not recognized the importance of incidental learning; in fact, it has either ignored it, on the one hand, or totally discounted it, on the other. Many persons are of the attitude that unless learning is planned, that is, you set out to learn some specific thing, you really haven't learned anything. And even worse, many persons believe that unless learning opportunities are offered by some institution, the learning somehow either is of lower quality or maybe is not learning at all. All this leads us to the next point.

Learning Is Living, and It Is Lifelong

Many persons want to separate learning from living, but doing this is impossible, for in many respects they are the same. As we live we learn. It is unavoidable. As we learn we live; how could it be otherwise? If learning is living and vice versa, then learning is, of course, lifelong. Learning is something we do from the first to the last moment of our lives. We may choose not to participate in planned learning all our lives, but this is a different argument.

Some people still believe that one learns in order to prepare for life and then one leads that life without needing further learning. A returning student wrote, "When I finished with my baccalaureate it was my firm belief that I would never set foot in a classroom again; that I was completely prepared for my career; that I would *never, ever* become a teacher; and that I would neither change my career nor would my chosen career betray me and require me to pursue additional education (I really assumed that I was safe!)" True, much of elementary, secondary, and higher education has a focus on preparing people for the future. But the day has long passed when it is even possible to consider that what you learned as a part of your formal schooling will be all that is necessary. Some observers claim that the professional training and knowledge of a graduate becomes obsolete 15 years or sooner after graduation unless the person's education is continuously updated through planned learning.[1] And this is likely a conservative estimate, for the knowledge available to and the skills required of many professionals change almost constantly. Most persons will change careers three or four times during their lifetimes, and in most instances considerable learning is required for each career change.

It is hard to imagine any person in today's society who could go through life without some planned learning. Society is changing too quickly. If for no other reason than to continue to be a well-informed citizen who can make intelligent choices in the voting booth, lifelong learning is a necessity.

Learning Is Problem Solving

One way people learn is by solving the many problems they face in their day-to-day living. Through the process of solving problems, you learn much—often without being totally aware that you are learning.

For example, let's assume that you hear the state is planning to relocate a major highway so that it will run through the heart of your neighborhood, which happens to be entirely residential. In organizing a citizen group to deal with this problem, you have a great potential for learning. You and your neighbors will learn how to organize a group. You will learn much about highway regulations, state laws on where highways may be located, what rights you as citizens have to protest such action, where resources to assist may be located, how to organize publicity campaigns, and so on. The situation is rich for learning, as are nearly all problem-solving situations.

A problem-solving situation may not be as elaborate as the one outlined above. It could be as simple as how to unstop a plugged sink. If everything you tried failed, you probably learned where to find a plumber to help with the problem.

Learning Is Reorganizing Experience

As an adult you bring to any learning situation many years of experience, which have resulted in much learning. When you face something new, you often have the task of reorganizing something you have learned previously. You think of a similar experience you had previously, and based on the new experience, you reorganize the old in the light of the new. It is often a very complex and difficult process, for most of us are quite protective of what we have learned previously. When we are faced with a new experience we are often reluctant to even pay any attention to it. Faced with a new learning experience—it may be a course we are taking, a workshop in which we are participating, some self-planned reading—we often meet ideas that run counter to what we have previously thought. Learning becomes a changing of the old in the light of the new, a reaffirming of the old when challenged by the new, and in some few instances a replacing of the old with the new.

Learning Is Often Unlearning

One of the differences between child and adult learning is the amount of unlearning the adult often faces. There are several ways to think about this problem: (1) You may have learned something that most people believed to be correct when you learned it, but research has since refuted this information. (2) You may have learned something incorrectly and never knew that what you learned was incorrect. More likely, (3) you may have learned something, but at the time you didn't explore in sufficient depth, and your conclusions might have been different had you gone deeper into the topic. Now, when you do go deeper into the topic, you find you must rethink your earlier conclusions. Still another situation, (4) you may have a conclusion, perhaps many years ago, based on some isolated experience in your life. Now when you are faced with a topic related to that experience, you find that your earlier conclusion from the experience was totally wrong.

Unlearning is not a pleasant task for most people. We do not like to give up something that is a part of us, which leads us to the next point.

Learning Can Be Joyous as Well as Painful

Unlearning something, as pointed out above, is often not a pleasant task. In fact, many times it can be quite painful: a person may believe something for many years and then in one short weekend have the idea challenged to the point where it must be changed. This kind of change can be trying and considerably less than joyous. Our memories of schooling are often painful as we recall the years of attending to what others insisted we learn.

On the other hand, learning can be joyous too. What could be more joyous than dealing with new ideas, fresh approaches to problems, new ways of thinking about old things. What could be more joyous than pushing yourself toward a potential you always knew was there but never came close to realizing. This is the joy of learning.

True, many instructors don't accept the idea that learning can be joyous and sometimes go out of their way to make it a sober, plodding experience. But it need not be so.

Often, learning is both joyous and painful. We feel the agony of having our old ideas challenged and at the same time the joy of stretching ourselves to reach new horizons. Learning, then, as pointed out earlier, is life, for life, too, has its agonies and its joys, its peaks and its valleys.

Learning Is Often Hard Work

One of the myths of adult learning is that it comes easy, that you don't have to work at it. Occasionally this is so, but not often. When you are engaged in learning something that is really important to you, you quickly find that it is hard work. But you may be so interested in what you are doing that you don't think so. It is at the end of class, after 2 hours of studying a challenging book, or after a debate with a friend over a point on which you disagree that you discover how exhausted you are. You didn't realize how hard you had been working. Of course, if you are learning something that is not particularly interesting to you, the work is even harder. This is no different from what happens with any other task you do but dislike.

Learning Is Growth

What is growth, you ask? It is reaching potentials: It is moving toward becoming what you have within you to become. It is moving toward realizing what you have the ability to realize.

Learning is a process, then, for helping you to become what you have the potential for becoming. And you will never get there. No matter how hard you study, no matter how many classes and courses you take, you will never completely realize your potential. You will always be striving toward it. This is of course the excitement of lifelong learning, which is open-ended, never completed. You can never learn everything you have the potential for learning. You can never achieve the growth you have the potential for achieving. On the other hand, you can always be more than you are now. Through purposeful and incidental learning, you can move closer to realizing your growth potential.

Since I have said all this about learning, you probably wonder why I didn't say anything about acquiring new information. Acquiring new information, to some people the beginning and the end of learning, is only one small part of the process. It is involved of course, but what you do with the information is the important thing. The main thing is how the information affects you, how it relates to experiences you have had, how it relates to a problem you face, and how it relates to other information you have. Simply acquiring information is the lowest level of learning.

BLOCKS TO LEARNING

With this overview of learning in mind, let's go on to explore some of the reasons why learning doesn't occur. To be more specific, as an adult learner, what are some of the blocks to your learning?

Attitude about Ability to Learn

You are one of the greatest blocks to your own learning. Your attitude about why you are studying, your ability to study, your self-concept as an adult student greatly influence how well you will learn. The logic goes like this. You feel unsure of yourself, which leads to anxiety when you face a formal learning situation, which in turn causes you to do poorly in a learning situation. This experience reinforces your earlier position of being unsure, and the circle is complete. In this crazy circle of despair, the true you as learner remains hidden by the anxious, unsure you. Not allowing your true self an opportunity to operate is a powerful block to learning.

A good example of this situation is the anxiety many returning learners have about mathematics. (Many universities are establishing remedial mathematics programs for returning students who anticipate problems with mathematics.) Math anxiety is particularly a problem for many women in our society. From grade school days on, women were subtly or sometimes not so subtly told that mathematics was for men and they would never do well with numbers.[2]

A woman responding to my survey about problems faced when returning to school wrote, "I was so petrified and so unsure of myself after being away from school for 8 years that I just worked very, very hard."

Her comments sum up the feelings of many adults who are once more enrolled in formal study. The attitude toward studying and learning may in part be traced back to the old myth that the older one gets the more difficult it is to learn.

The attitude also has roots in the policy that education prepares young people for the life they will live when they finish school. As an adult, you are now supposed to be living that life. The idea of returning to school runs counter to this long-held belief and may subconsciously get in the way of your learning.

J. R. Kidd, a Canadian adult educator, has studied and written about this question for many years. His findings are revealing.

In general, as we grow older we slow down. That is likely not news to you, particularly if you are over 40. This slowing down takes many forms. Your blood flows more slowly through your veins and arteries. "Messages" pass more slowly through your nervous system. The time necessary for damage to your body to be repaired is longer than when you were a child.

Insofar as learning processes are concerned, you perceive more slowly, think more slowly, and learn more slowly as you grow older.

Your ability to see and to hear also decreases with age. Your ability to see increases rapidly during early childhood, and there is a slow but continuous gain between the ages of 13 and 18. From your eighteenth birthday until your fortieth year, there is a general, slow and gradual decline. From age 40 to age 55 there is a sharp decline, and then there is a steady decline after that, but at a decreased rate. Beginning after age 18, on the average, one's field of vision also narrows and the ability to adapt to the dark is slower.

These figures are, of course, based on averages. Many persons do not wear glasses at age 45, but many more do than don't. Some people aren't aware of this rather normal decline in visual functioning and let the decline affect their attitude toward learning.

A similar decrease in functioning occurs with hearing. The peak hearing performance appears to be reached around age 15, with a gradual decline until about age 65. Not only is there a gradual decline in the ability to hear at all, but one also hears more slowly as one grows older. It takes us longer to translate the meaning of sounds and to respond to them as we grow older.

Maybe even more so than does seeing, hearing affects our attitudes toward learning. If we find that we have lost some of our ability to hear, we conclude too quickly that we have also lost some of our ability to learn.

Our reaction time, the time it takes us to respond to something, also slows. For example, as we get older it takes us longer to move our foot from the accelerator to the brake pedal when we are driving. It also takes us longer to respond to such things as multiple-choice questions in timed examinations.

As we get older, in summary, our ability to see and hear decreases and there is a general slowing down. Most of us have learned how to cope with any decrease in ability to see and hear, although we may still believe that this decrease in functioning has something to do with how we learn.[3] But we haven't learned how to deal with the general slowing down that all of us experience as we grow older. This gives us the most problems because our society is one that is essentially based on speed and efficiency. Getting more done in less time has been the spoken and unspoken motto in this country for many years. It has become a part of most of us. If we find that there are activities we can't do as rapidly as someone else can, some of us tend to avoid these activities. Learning is one of the activities in which we slow down as we get older.

Unfortunately, many institutions in which you will be studying have not taken into account the fact that people learn more slowly as they grow older. If you find yourself in a situation where, for example, you are expected to take timed examinations or everyone is expected to learn at the same rate, you will be frustrated. And you have good reason to be. In the last chapter of this book we discuss some of the things you can reasonably expect to be changed if institutions are going to adjust to large numbers of older students.

What you need to insist on, as an older student, is the opportunity to choose your own pace for learning and to have sufficient time available to accomplish the learning tasks expected of you.

All of what I've been talking about may sound more than a little depressing to you. But I'd like to end this section on a high note. Notice that nothing I've said so far in this discussion about the adult learner has related to ability to learn. Our society, with its extreme emphasis on time and efficiency, has confused *rate* of learning and *ability* to learn. The assumption has been that if rate of learning has decreased then ability to learn has decreased as well. The two things must be separated. Just because you learn less rapidly as you grow older does not mean that your ability to learn has decreased. In fact, a case can be made that as you get older your ability to learn increases, particularly in certain areas. For example, research evidence suggests that verbal intelligence increases with age, at least until the midfifties, for intellectually active adults.[4] Thus ability to learn in areas requiring verbal ability increases with age for many persons. It can be argued that the accumulated experiences of living are a considerable asset to you as an adult learner. As you face new experiences, you can often relate parts or all of the new experience to something you have experienced previously.

The Learner's Family's Attitude

As you already know, I'm sure, there is still some considerable stigma attached to adult study, particularly when it is full-time study.

One adult student responding to the questionnaire about problems in returning to school noted: "I had the disadvantage of not having moral support from anyone. My family and friends thought it was pretty ridiculous to go on in school. I already had a master's degree; why didn't I just go find a good job? And even after several semesters back in school, I still don't feel completely 'legitimate.' "

The support of the immediate family, particularly one's spouse, is essential to success as an adult student. Of course, if your family and friends are bombarding you with comments about how foolish it is to pursue additional study, you must be of a strong mind to not let these comments affect your attitude toward study and learning. There is always the tendency to believe that maybe these people are right, that maybe you shouldn't be going off on this adventure of once more becoming a student.

Attitude toward the Process of Learning

Adults returning to formal study after many years away from school often bring unpleasant memories with them. They remember the long, often boring hours they spent cooped up behind a desk on warm spring days and cool, crisp fall afternoons when a walk in the woods, anything outdoors, would be more pleasant than the schoolroom. You may have memories of some teachers who insisted on directing your learning so you had little, if any, freedom to do what you wanted to do, to learn some of the things you wanted to learn. You probably remember—and not too positively either—the many exams you sweated over, the anxious hours you spent preparing for them, and the questions that asked for the regurgitation of facts rather than for understanding.

And you probably remember, too, teachers telling some children that they were not students and would likely never be—that they should seek some line of work for which study would not be important. This was the most cruel of comments. It is obvious today that all of us will be students all our lives. Some of our "study time" will be spent in schools and colleges when we are adults, but much of it will be spent in in-service sessions where we work, in self-study programs we put together for ourselves, and in noncredit classes and courses we may enroll in. There is no such thing as not having the potential for becoming a student. In fact the comment is irrelevant. Whether we believe it or not, we are and must be continuing learners all of our lives. We are students constantly.

What happened to us as elementary and high school students and maybe as college students too has a great effect on our attitude toward learning today. Great strides are being made to make learning situations for adults not like those some adults experienced as youngsters.

Attitude toward Learning and Life

It is a rather common assumption held by many people in our society that one learns in particular places, in classrooms that are a part of educational institutions, for example. Of course there is great potential for learning in classrooms, but there is great potential for learning almost everywhere we happen to be. The problem is that we often try to separate learning from life; we try to place learning in a box (classroom). By doing this, we deny the richness of learning experiences that we face every day. By boxing learning experiences, we often overlook or fail to take advantage of the rich experiences we encounter constantly and fail to learn as much from them as we might.

This separation of learning from life of course affects our overall attitude toward learning. It makes us think far too narrowly. It causes us to approach planned learning experiences—those that are conducted in classrooms—as if they were somehow not part of our lives.

If we start with the attitude that learning is something we do every day of our lives, that some of it is planned and much of it is incidental, and that some of it is sponsored by institutions but all of it may not be, we can then see learning as an integral part of our lives. We can see learning as really no different from eating or sleeping—a need we have as part of living. We can begin to view learning as living and living as learning.

Problems in Adjusting

Persons who have been out of formal education for several years and are returning often experience an assortment of problems associated with becoming a student again. The majority of the students (60 percent) who responded to my informal questionnaire said that it took them about one semester to adjust to study and student life. Of course all these students were adults who had returned to full-time study at a university. And most of them were graduate students, which means that at some time in their formal study they had already spent a minimum of 4 years at a college or university. Still they had adjustment problems that weren't solved until the first semester of their return to school had essentially passed.

What were some of these problems? Many of the problems were the topics we are covering in this book: how to use resources, how to write exams, how to read more efficiently, how to write term papers, how to study, how to use time more effectively, how to adjust to younger and often more inexperienced students attending the same classes, how to adjust to professors who didn't seem to understand that you had spent several years working and often had another perspective to contribute to a class.

There were other adjustment problems too. For example, one returning student wrote:

> When I arrived in Madison the most distressing problem was finding an apartment with the help of the Sunday want ads and a map of the city. Every street I wanted to use was one way in the opposite direction from my intended destina-

tion. Running a close second was finding buildings on campus the first week. It took me a month to work up enough courage to search for something in Memorial Library. My son encouraged me to use it and assured me that the tales of students who disappear into the stacks, never to be heard of again, were just local folklore.

Another student wrote:

I think I am sometimes distracted from my studies as an adult by such concerns as money, by societal disapproval of goals that seem presumptuous for a middle-aged woman, and by domestic problems that drift through my mind as I try to study something like statistics, which for me requires total concentration. The figures I am dealing with are supposed to represent the association between the poverty rates and crime rates in neighborhoods. But my mind skips to figures on my complicated, goofed-up joint income tax return with my estranged (and solvent) husband. Sometimes when I study I think about my adult sons and wonder if they are safe. These distractions may be no worse than the ones I had when I was 17 at Penn State. Then I was distracted by the problems of whether or not I'd be invited to a fraternity party. When I was invited I was distracted by thoughts of what I ought to wear. Right now these seem like small concerns, but they did serve to take my mind from my assignments. In this regard I think perhaps adult and younger learners are not too different. The importance of my decisions, however, seems very great to me right now. It is as though I have no room for error any more, which is a heavy strain.

Still another student replied:

What probably would have helped me most is the information that readjustment to the academic situation is a problem experienced by many returning students and is not unique to myself. Knowing this might have helped to relieve some of the frustration I felt.

So the adjustment problem, as viewed by students, is very real. And it has many dimensions, as illustrated by the above comments.

Some of the students resented certain kinds of adjustments they were required to make. "I was ill prepared to be treated with such disrespect, condescension, etc., from egocentric professors." Refer to the last chapter of this book for a discussion of many of these kinds of concerns and what you as a returning student might do about them.

Time Constraints

No other block to learning is mentioned more often by adults returning to school than insufficient time. This is understandable. Many adult students are working full time while they study part time. Most of them have family responsibilities, and often community responsibilities, in addition to their work schedule. Within this complex of time requirements must be placed time for attending classes and, even more important, time for study. This problem of finding study time often seems insurmountable, but there are ways to deal with it.

Keep a Time Inventory   One easy thing to do is a time inventory. For a week record how you spend your time, from when you get up in the morning until you go to bed at night. (Use the time inventory form for this purpose.) Record your job hours if you are working. Record your class time and study time. Write down the times you spend commuting to work and to class, and the time you spend eating. Record the time you spend with your family.

Once you have done this for a week, you can begin to see certain patterns of time use. And you can begin to question how you use your time and the priorities you place on your time use. For instance, have you set enough time aside for study?

Try a Weekly Time Plan   Once you have completed your time inventory and have made some decisions, do a weekly time plan. (Use the weekly time plan form.) If you have a family, let them in on your plans and ask for their support. The time you set aside for study is protected. It is yours and is not to be disturbed.

Be realistic about planning study time. It is generally better to have 2 hours of study time every day than an entire half day a week set aside for study. Generally you will accomplish more with several shorter study periods. And make sure that in your schedule you plan time for your family and time for recreation.

Along with planning must go discipline. If you have planned an hour of study time each morning at five o'clock, then you must discipline yourself to study each morning at that time. You'll find that you will carry on an interesting conversation with yourself until you have gotten into the routine of everyday study. One part of you will insist that you owe yourself another hour of sleep and that you don't really need to get up to study. The other part of you will argue that you must stick to your plans.

I'm reminded of what professional writers do. They, too, must struggle with the problem of disciplining themselves and sticking to a schedule if they are going to be productive. Many professional writers write every day whether they feel like writing or not. They do not wait for an inspiration, as some people believe. They sit in front of their typewriters and write, as painful as that is on some days. The same disciplined approach applies to you as a student. Whether you feel like it or not, you must stick to your plan. It is the hours spent studying each day that in the long run

TIME INVENTORY WORKSHEET

	Sunday	Monday	Tuesday	Wednesday	Thursday	Friday	Saturday
6:00 A.M.							
7:00 A.M.							
8:00 A.M.							
9:00 A.M.							
10:00 A.M.							
11:00 A.M.							
12:00 M.							
1:00 P.M.							
2:00 P.M.							
3:00 P.M.							
4:00 P.M.							
5:00 P.M.							
6:00 P.M.							
7:00 P.M.							
8:00 P.M.							
9:00 P.M.							
10:00 P.M.							
11:00 P.M.							
12:00 P.M.							

WEEKLY TIME PLAN

	Sunday	Monday	Tuesday	Wednesday	Thursday	Friday	Saturday
6:00 A.M.							
7:00 A.M.							
8:00 A.M.							
9:00 A.M.							
10:00 A.M.							
11:00 A.M.							
12:00 M.							
1:00 P.M.							
2:00 P.M.							
3:00 P.M.							
4:00 P.M.							
5:00 P.M.							
6:00 P.M.							
7:00 P.M.							
8:00 P.M.							
9:00 P.M.							
10:00 P.M.							
11:00 P.M.							
12:00 P.M.							

will determine your success as a student. Though some students seem to be successful in passing examinations through last-minute cramming, this does not lead to the most productive learning. Day-by-day, ordinary, disciplined study will in the long run help you learn more, keep you caught up with your assignments, and incidently also provide you with what you need in order to pass examinations.

If you do find that you have 2- or 3-hour blocks of time in which you can study, you might do what John Muir, the famous naturalist, did when he studied. Many persons do not know that John Muir was also an inventor. One of his many inventions was a special study desk connected to a clock. After he had spent approximately 50 minutes of study at his desk, a device was set into motion that picked up the book he was studying and set another in front of him. Muir's theory was that he should not work on any one topic for longer than an hour at a time. His theory makes sense. After an hour of study in one subject, award yourself a 15-minute break before returning to your desk. You will be fresher and more productive.

Use Spare Moments Another way of handling the time problem is to *become a student 5 minutes at a time.* Carry note cards with you in your pocket or purse, and when you are waiting for the bus, waiting at the dentist's office, waiting to see your academic adviser—wherever you happen to be during your busy day when there are 5 spare minutes—think about what you have been studying and note down the important points. Carrying one of your textbooks with you is also a time-saving suggestion. When you have a spare moment, read. These fleeting study moments cannot take the place of more concentrated study periods, but they can add up. Three 5 minute study periods a day for 5 days add up to 1 hour and 15 minutes, time that otherwise would have been lost.

Keep a "To Do" List Still another technique for managing time and priorities is a daily "to do" list. A to do list is a listing of all the things you want to accomplish for the day, including personal activities, as well as work-, family-, and school-related activities. Place an asterisk in front of those items that are of highest priority. When a task is completed, cross it off. If a task is not completed, enter it on the next day's to do list.

Some people find it more convenient to have a weekly to do list rather than one for each day. You will need to decide which is more convenient for you. Most persons also find it convenient to have their to do list written on cards or in a notebook small enough to carry in their pocket or purse. This same card or notebook can also be used to record upcoming to do items that you learn about during the course of a day.

A sample to do list might look this way:

To do: **Wednesday**

*1 Study for psychology exam
*2 Start reading for sociology paper
 3 Take Mary to dentist at 4:00
*4 Prepare presentation for board meeting
 5 Pay car insurance premium
 6 Make an appointment with Mary's teacher
*7 See Professor Carlyle about missing class next week

Keep a Monthly Calendar   Keeping a monthly calendar helps to keep all the academic tasks to be performed in some sort of perspective. What works best is one of the large calendars with enough space to write on each date. Here record such things as upcoming examinations, and dates when papers are due. Many families already keep calendars of this type. If you have a family and you have such a family calendar, it is a simple matter to add to it those deadlines that relate to your student work. Perhaps you will want to write your student deadlines in a different color ink, to set them off from such items as appointments or who is driving in the car pool this week.

Inability to Concentrate

Many returning students tell me they are able, after some careful planning, to set aside blocks of time for study. But then, when they have the time, they aren't able to concentrate. They tell me they can't keep their minds from roaming widely, from ill children to problems at work—a thousand thoughts that churn and turn. They tell me they sometimes can't read for more than 5 minutes before the rush of other thoughts prevents them from going on.

Following are some tips to help with concentration. Unfortunately there are no magic cures. But returning students tell me these tips have helped. They also tell me that with attention to improving concentration, it does improve even though the improvement may take a month or so.

1 *Assign a Time for Study*   I talked about this in the previous section and want to underline it here. Concentration is aided considerably if you know that at certain hours each day you will be studying. Let your family know this too. Tell them that during your assigned study time you don't want to be bothered.

2 *Provide Some Flexibility* This will sound like a contradiction of number 1. But there will be times when you must do something other than study during your assigned study times. This is to be expected. What you do is trade another time so you end up with the same amount of time.

3 *Set Aside a Study Place* Concentration is aided if you have a place where you study only. You don't write bills there, you don't read novels there, you don't play with the kids there. You only study there. It need not be a fancy place. All that is necessary is a good light, a flat place to spread out your books and papers, and a good straight-backed chair.

I recall when I came back to school. My wife and I talked about a study place and we agreed the section of our basement where we stored the storm windows might serve the purpose. We carried the storm windows to the garage, swept down the cobwebs, and strung in an extension cord for a desk light. An old door with legs screwed on the corners served as a desk. It was quiet, out of the way, and a place where I studied, and that's all. The kids knew to stay away from "daddy's corner," so study materials could be left in place from one study time to the next.

4 *Use Study Breaks* Study for an hour, then take a 15-minute break. Knowing that you will have a break is in itself an aid to concentration. If you have other things to think about, you know you can do it during the break. Concentrate as fully as you can during your assigned study time, then, during the break, leave your study place and do something entirely different. Don't even think about what you are studying.

5 *Study Your Most Difficult Subjects when You Are Fresh* If you are a morning person, study your difficult subjects during your morning study times. Save your afternoon study times for more routine tasks such as reorganizing your lecture notes, or organizing research material for a paper.

6 *Set Goals and Keep a Study Record* One way to increase your concentration level is to set study goals and then keep a record of your accomplishments. Use the form below to record dates and times, study goals and study accomplishments. For instance you might, for a given study time, plan to read ten pages of an assigned reading and at the end of

STUDY RECORD

Date	Time	Study goal	Accomplished

the time discover you had completed eight pages. Record keeping of this sort can help you evaluate your study behavior. And by increasing your study goals over achievements, you can move yourself toward greater study accomplishment, and likely better concentration, too.

7 *Use a Reminder Pad*   If you are distracted by thinking about other things that need to be done while you are studying, keep a notepad on your desk and write down the items. Then go back to studying. With the items written down you know you won't forget them, and they won't keep popping into your head and destroying your concentration.

8 *Balance Study Time with Other Activities*   For those who are working full time or have families, this suggestion will take care of itself. But for those who are able to go to school full time there is such a thing as too much study. Break it up. Jog around the block. Play tennis. Go to a movie. Read a good novel. Do anything that is a contrast to studying. You'll find you are much more likely to concentrate when you do study, if your life is varied.

Inability to See Wholes

In part this block to learning is related to the problem of insecurity that many returning adults bring with them. When we are feeling insecure we want to get on with the task, to finish it quickly, for fear that we might not be able to do it. In our haste we often concentrate on the facts of the situation and don't take the necessary time to attempt to put the facts into some kind of perspective. Seeing the whole picture means seeing how the facts you are studying relate to some larger whole, how the books you are reading contribute to the course you are studying, how the various topics presented by the instructor fit together into a whole, and even more important, how all the courses you are taking fit into your life.

Searching for wholes, which may at the beginning seem to steal valuable time away from "learning" facts, will in the long run make everything easier for you. Searching for wholes is searching for meaning, and a search for meaning is an important part of learning.

You search for wholes by constantly asking where individual bits of information fit; what the main point of the instructor's lecture was; what, in overview, a book is about.

The process of searching for wholes is facilitated when you relax and do not worry about not finishing a study assignment on time or doing poorly on an examination. Figuratively speaking, you must back up a few steps from the course and classes, books and notes, and professors and fellow students and ask what it is all about, what the big picture is. This you must do often to keep all the new information you are dealing with in perspective.

To help you begin to focus on wholes, write the answers to the following questions:

1 What are your academic goals? _____

_____

_____

_____

2 What are your personal goals? _____

_____

_____

_____

3 How does each course you are now taking relate to your goals?
Course A: Title of course _____

_____

_____

Course B: Title of course _____

_____

_____

Course C: Title of course _____

_____

_____

Course D: Title of course _____

_____

_____

LEARNING HOW TO LEARN

Now that we've given you some insights into what learning is, what the blocks to learning are, and how to work at overcoming them, we are ready to talk about that somewhat elusive concept *learning how to learn*.

At the beginning of this chapter we said that learning how to learn could be defined as taking charge of your own learning. Now let's be more specific as to how you might go about doing that.

Several writers and researchers in adult education have been interested in the concept of learning how to learn. If you wish to pursue the topic beyond the brief explanation presented here, refer to the list of suggested readings at the end of this chapter.

We may look at learning how to learn from two perspectives, the skills necessary for learning and the process of learning how to learn. The skills necessary are the major topics that make up this book: study skills such as taking exams, listening, taking notes, and the like; thinking both logically and creatively; reading effectively, depending on the type of material and the purposes for reading; improving vocabulary; and increasing writing skills.

Now we will turn our attention to the process of learning how to learn.

The Process of Learning How to Learn

As we have pointed out above, the process of learning how to learn is based on the assumption that you the adult learner will have a considerable input into your own learning. This is of course a shift away from the more traditional way of thinking about teaching and learning, in which you as the learner were dependent on someone else to plan, carry out, and evaluate your learning. The process of learning how to learn may be frustrating to you, particularly if you haven't done it before and if you wonder if you should do it. Malcolm Knowles summarizes the problem well when he writes, "It is a tragic fact that most of us only know how to be taught; we haven't learned how to learn."[5] Most of our learning experiences, particularly those related to formal schooling, are related to being taught. We have little input into the process used.

The process of learning how to learn involves three stages: (1) planning, (2) carrying out, and (3) evaluating. In the simplest of terms, you decide what you want to do, you do it, and then you determine how effective you have been.

1 **Planning** During this stage you determine the problem or question you want answered. You determine your learning needs.

Your learning needs may be at various levels. You may have determined that you need an advanced degree so that you can progress in your professional field. You may have decided to change careers, to do something entirely different with your life, and your new choice of career requires that you do considerable study. Your community may be facing several problems, and you want to help work on them but you feel inadequate. You want to improve your ability to assist with community problem solving. You may want to learn a specific skill such as typewriting or swimming or public speaking. You may have heard about a new approach to energy conservation, and you want to learn more about it. You may have always wanted to learn more about the Old Testament or perhaps about Plato or Emerson or Thoreau. All these reasons can be bases for planning.

During the planning stage you may feel comfortable and competent planning by yourself. But it is likely that you will need some assistance, particularly if you have identified a learning need in an area that is somewhat foreign to you. For example, if you are planning a career change you may not know what information you need to become competent in a new area. Someone who is in that area can help you. Reading books about that area may help you. Talking to someone responsible for training programs in that area may be helpful to you. Even though you are seeking help from others, you are making the final decisions—you are developing your own plan. Someone may try to map out the plan for you, may tell you what you need to know. You must be comfortable enough and confident enough to talk with others about what has been suggested and then, when you have as much information as you can find, make your own learning plan.

Be as specific with your learning plan as you can be at this stage. Actually write down some learning objectives, some specific things you want to learn. If you want to learn typewriting, the task is fairly easy. You might write, ''I want to be able to type 40 words a minute.'' If you are returning to school to advance in your profession, you may identify some specific skills and knowledge that you believe you need to learn for that advancement to take place. Realize, too, that once you begin your learning project, no matter how brief or how extensive it may be, you may change many of your learning objectives during the process of learning. The entire process of learning how to learn is flexible and open to change. And it *should* be for the learning to be most effective for your purposes.

Once you have determined your goals for the present time, you are ready to ask: How can I meet these learning objectives? Where are the resources that will help me to do this? You may discover that a book in the library is the only resource you need to meet a particular learning objective you have identified for yourself. On the other hand, you may identify that 3 years of graduate study at a major university is what is required to meet your learning objectives. In between these two extremes, you may identify courses to take, workshops to attend, independent-study courses to pursue, and individuals with whom you may talk to meet your learning objectives. Often you will identify some combination of activities. At the same time that you are pursuing formal study at a university, you may want to talk with persons who are practicing what you are preparing for. You may want to supplement formal credit course work with noncredit workshops. Usually some mix of activities provides a richer experience than only one approach.

Three activities make up the planning phase of learning how to learn:

a Determining learning needs
b Identifying learning objectives
c Identifying resources to meet objectives

The planning stage actually goes on throughout the time you are carrying out your learning project. For example, once you have determined that you want to pursue another degree at a university, then you begin planning again. What courses will you take? Most programs of formal study have considerable flexibility in terms of courses that may be taken. The courses that are actually taken in a formal degree program are often determined by the student and the student's academic adviser.

And as mentioned above, once you begin study in an area, you may find that you want to revise your learning objectives or add additional ones. You may discover an area for further inquiry and may want to revise your learning objectives accordingly. This is not to imply that you let whim direct your learning. Indeed not. Planning your learning is a kind of tension between holding fast to your original plan, on the one hand, and being open to promising learning opportunities that present themselves as you involve yourself in learning, on the other hand. Constantly planning is part of the excitement of learning, particularly when you have control of the process.

2   Carrying Out   As the label implies, this phase of the process is the doing phase. You enroll in classes; you take part in independent study; you talk with resource people. Here is where the various study skills that this book discusses can be put to good use. Your goal is to be an effective and an efficient learner. You want to get as much as possible from the learning activities you have selected. Part of the responsibility is yours. If you are pursuing formal course work, you must know how to use the various learning resources available on campus, such as the library and the staff. Your reading, writing, thinking, and study skills must be honed to a sharpness that allows you to learn effectively and confidently.

Two activities are included in the carrying out phase:

a Getting in touch with learning resources
b Sharpening learning skills

Not always are the resources that you have selected, whether they be human resources such as instructors in courses or nonhuman resources such as books and films of the quality to fit your needs, exactly related to the learning objectives that you have established for yourself.

This leads us to the next phase of the process, evaluation.

3   Evaluation   In many ways it is inappropriate to establish evaluation as the third phase of learning how to learn. One very important evaluative effort goes on all the time. It is evaluation when you constantly ask yourself if your learning objectives continue to be appropriate. It is evaluation when you make judgments about an instructor in a course and decide to drop the course because either the course is not directly related to your needs or the instructor does not meet your expectations. It is evaluation when you read a book in overview and then decide that for your purposes, it makes no sense to read any more of that book.

Evaluation may be described in two ways: evaluation that occurs during the actual process of learning and evaluation that occurs at the end of some learning project. Above, we have described some examples of evaluation that occurs during the learning process. When you have completed a learning project, you also want to do some evaluation to determine if your learning objectives have been met. You want to determine if the skills and the knowledge you wanted to gain have indeed been gained. You want to determine how effective you have been in your learning effort.

Now we must stop for a minute and look at a conflict that exists within this broad topic of learning evaluation. The issue revolves around the question of who should do the evaluation. From the examples given above, you could quickly assume that evaluation is your responsibility as a learner. Yet you will find many persons who, in instructor-led learning activities, believe that it is the instructor who has the responsibility for determining if one has learned. This is of course the traditional way of doing evaluation, the approach to evaluation that you likely remember from your formal school days. This is the approach that involves examinations and grades, curves and comparisons, and competition among students.

The conflict of who should evaluate is not going to be resolved in these few pages, for many articles have been written on the topic. For our purposes, as we emphasize the concept of learning how to learn, it seems logical that you the learner should have a major say in determining how you are doing. In many ways it would seem totally out of place to suggest that an outsider could evaluate how well you are meeting your learning objectives. At best this outside evaluator could evaluate how well you were reaching the objectives that he or she thought you should be reaching.

The issue becomes more complicated when we inject into the argument the question of standards and certification. You may be pursuing study that will lead to preparing you for a profession; let's say it is to become a social science researcher. Among social scientists there is some broad agreement that researchers in the field need to have certain skills and that they must have achieved these skills at certain levels; that is, they must have achieved a certain standard. In this case, because the learner is entering an arena where he or she may have had difficulty making much personal input into the specific learning objectives at the outset, without some outside assistance he or she will also have difficulty in determining if the learning objectives have been reached.

Unfortunately, though, many professional educators believe that the learner has no role in evaluation: that evaluation is *done to* the learner. It is this position we are challenging. You as an adult learner who is trying to gain more control over your learning must also strive to gain control over the evaluation of that learning. You may require assistance in certain instances and may even be evaluated by an outside process in some isolated cases. But you should strive to gain control of the evaluation of your own learning.

Evaluation should help you to adjust the learning process as it goes along. This statement would apply to a 3-year degree program or to a 2-session workshop. Evaluation should help you to evaluate the extent to which you have reached the learning objectives you have set down for yourself. After accomplishing evaluation you should have some idea about what you want to do next. If you have not sufficiently accomplished some of your learning objectives, then you may want to pursue them further, perhaps using some different learning resources.

The evaluation process includes three activities:

a Determining if adjustments in learning activities are necessary
b Determining if learning objectives have been met
c Determining follow-up activities

The learning-how-to-learn process in total includes the following phases and steps:

1 Planning
   a Determining learning needs
   b Identifying learning objectives
   c Identifying resources to meet objectives
2 Carrying out
   a Getting in touch with learning resources
   b Sharpening learning skills
3 Evaluation
   a Determining if adjustments in learning activities are necessary
   b Determining if learning objectives have been met
   c Determining follow-up activities

SUMMARY

In this chapter we have considered three broad topics: what learning is, blocks to learning, and the process of learning how to learn. We said that learning is doing; learning is change; learning can be planned or incidental; learning is living and is lifelong; learning is problem solving; learning is reorganizing experience; learning is often unlearning; learning can be joyous as well as painful; learning is often hard work; and learning is growth.

Blocks to learning include attitude about ability to learn, learner's family's attitude, attitude toward the process of learning, attitude toward learning and life, problems in adjusting, time constraints, concentration, and inability to see wholes.

Learning how to learn was discussed as a goal for adult learners. The idea is built on the premise that adults will take charge of their own learning. This is not to imply that they won't take courses and that they won't often relate to a wide array of learning resources, but ultimately the adult learner will make the decisions about his or her learning. Three broad phases of learning how to learn were discussed: (1) planning, (2) carrying out, and (3) evaluation. All three phases often occur at the same time as a learner works toward meeting some learning need he or she has identified.

REFERENCES

1 Theodore M. Hesburgh, Paul A. Miller, and Clifton R. Wharton, Jr., *Patterns for Lifelong Learning,* Jossey-Bass, San Francisco, 1973.
2 Sheila Tobias, "Math Anxiety: Why Is a Smart Girl Like You Counting on Your Fingers?" *Ms.,* vol. V, no. 1, September 1976, pp. 56–59.
3 J. R. Kidd, *How Adults Learn,* Association Press, New York, 1973.
4 Leona Tyler, *Individual Differences, Abilities and Motivational Direction,* Appleton, New York, 1974; and *The Psychology of Human Differences,* Appleton, New York, 1965.
5 Malcolm Knowles, *Self-Directed Learning,* Association Press, New York, 1975.

CHAPTER 2

TAKING NOTES, LISTENING, AND TAKING EXAMINATIONS

In the last chapter we discussed a process for learning how to learn. The remainder of this book will focus on helping you improve those skills necessary in carrying out the process.

When you return to school you will quickly become aware that many learning opportunities are available to you. If you are one who "stopped out" of college several years ago and is now returning, you will likely be surprised at the variety of opportunities now available.

Traditional colleges and universities depended for years on lecture classes and, in the science areas, on lecture classes combined with laboratory experiences. These of course still exist and are important learning opportunities at every college and university. Many other opportunities exist as well. Some of these were available 10 years ago; some were not. Some of the opportunities discussed below were available but few students took advantage of them. Expect to find most, if not all, of the following learning opportunities available to you.

LEARNING OPPORTUNITIES

Traditional Lecture

As mentioned above, the traditional lecture, in which the professor stands in front of the class for 50 minutes and gives a speech, is still a popular and useful learning opportunity. With the advent of audiovisual technology in the past several years, many professors use slides, films, and overhead visual aids in addition to the traditional chalkboard to illustrate their lectures. Later in this chapter we will discuss skills that will help you make the most of lecture courses you attend.

Lecture-Discussion

This may be a new form of teaching for you. A professor shares several ideas, then stops for a discussion of those ideas with the class. In many of the smaller classes, those up to fifty in size, professors often use this instructional approach. Not only do you have a chance to be exposed to new information, but also you have an opportunity to ask questions and discuss the information with the professor and other students in the class.

Discussion

On some campuses small groups of students meet with an instructor in what are called *quiz sections*. Often discussion groups are formed from large lecture classes, giving students an opportunity to ask questions about what was presented during the lecture. Some courses, however, are organized entirely around the discussion approach, in which the instructor serves as discussion leader. Usually a considerable amount of reading is done outside of class and class time is used for discussion of what has been read.

Seminar

The seminar is a popular form of instruction at the graduate level and is occasionally used at the undergraduate level. It is different from the discussion approach because the seminar participants are themselves responsible for the various seminar sessions. Usually each student has responsibility for at least one seminar session during a semester. This approach gives much responsibility to the students for planning, presenting, and leading the seminar discussion.

Laboratory

Used heavily in science courses, to a lesser extent in social science courses, but also considerably in language courses, laboratory sessions allow students to practice what they are studying. Most returning students are quite familiar with the laboratory approach to instruction because of their experiences in elementary and high school.

Informal Discussion

Because it is not led by an instructor, the informal discussion is often overlooked as a learning opportunity. The informal discussion consists of a group of students who assemble on their own to discuss what they are studying in a given course. Occasionally the informal discussion can regress into a gripe session if students allow it. But when it is properly planned and conducted, the informal discussion can be one of the most valuable of any learning opportunity available to you. It does require effort and time on the part of students, however.

Independent Study

There are two forms of independent study, that which is guided and that which is self-directed. In guided independent study the student works with a professor over a given time period, say, a semester. A student may identify a question area in which he or she has an interest, but no particular course deals with the question in depth. Together with an instructor, the student may select a reading list and may identify some people to be interviewed. (Guided independent study takes a variety of forms.)

Several times during the semester the student meets with the professor to discuss progress. The student may also be asked to prepare a paper summarizing the results of the effort.

Another form of guided independent study is commonly known as *correspondence study*. Many colleges and universities, through their extension or continuing education divisions, offer courses by mail. The student completes assignments that are then evaluated by an instructor who communicates by letter with the student. Occasionally correspondence study is combined with one or more face-to-face meetings of the instructor and the student to discuss the student's progress.

In nonguided study students, entirely on their own, plan and carry out personal learning programs. For instance, a student may decide to study her home state's history. She may go to the library, perhaps consult with the librarian, and select several books. She may also decide to spend an hour or two visiting with persons at the state historical society to get more leads on how she might further her inquiry. She may talk to a professor who specializes in local history. She is obtaining help from others, but no one person is guiding the overall learning experience. For this the student has taken responsibility.

Allen Tough, in his research, reports that among the adult population of our country about 70 percent of all deliberate adult learning is self-directed.[1] Dr. Tough's research includes adults who are involved in systematic learning projects.

Internship

This is best described as guided learning on the job. Many colleges and universities, at both the undergraduate and the graduate levels, provide students the opportunity to work in the area for which they are preparing and to receive credit for it. Sometimes they also receive a salary.

Student engineers spend time working in an engineering firm; agricultural business majors work in an agricultural business; and prospective community developers work in a community development agency.

Usually two types of supervision are involved in the internship experience. The immediate supervisor for the student is the person in the agency or business to which the student is assigned. The academic supervisor is the student's major professor or adviser.

An internship experience, correctly designed, allows students to actually work at—to practice—what they are preparing to do. It also allows students time to reflect about and discuss with both the work adviser and the academic adviser what the students are doing, what problems they are experiencing, and perhaps what further academic training is necessary.

In addition to providing students the opportunity to practice what they are learning in their classes and courses, the internship experience helps many students make certain decisions. After spending 6 months or a year working in an agency or a business, a student has an excellent perspective as to whether or not that type of work is really what is wanted.

BASIC STUDY SKILLS

For each of these learning opportunities, certain basic study skills will help you gain more from the opportunity. These skills include reading, writing, thinking, listening, taking notes, and taking examinations. Succeeding chapters will discuss reading, writing, and thinking. The remainder of this chapter will look at how to improve your note-taking, listening, and exam-taking skills.

Taking Notes

Note taking is one of the most effective ways to become an active listener. By this time in your life you have likely worked out some kind of system for taking notes when you listen to someone talk. You may carry a small notebook to meetings and public lectures or you may write on the back of an envelope or on the side of the meeting's printed program. For some of you note taking is not a problem; others of you wonder if there is a better way to do it.

Since the lightweight cassette tape recorder with a built-in microphone that picks up voices at a distance has been invented, you are probably wondering why we are discussing note taking. Why not buy a cassette recorder and a sack full of tapes and tape all the lectures you attend? Then you can go back and listen to them at your leisure, as many times as you want to.

There are times when recording a lecture is an excellent idea. If you are enrolled in a course in which the content is technical and new to you, it is probably a good idea to record the lectures. If as a new returning student, you are somewhat unsure of your note-taking ability, you may want to record some of the first lectures in a course until your note-taking skills and confidence return.

Generally it is *not* a good idea to depend on the tape recorder as a substitute for note taking. Several things, mostly bad, can happen if you do. You may find yourself not listening to the lecture but allowing your mind to wander to other topics. You may rationalize that the recorder is capturing the information, so why bother to listen. Of course you will lose all the nonverbal communication clues that the lecturer offers. And you probably also will lose the sense of where the visual material that is presented on the chalkboard or on the screen fits into the sequence of the content. You will lose the opportunity to interact with the material as it is presented, to relate it to material you've read and to experiences you've had. True, you could carry out this step later when you listened to the tape. This leads to the last problem. How many students have the time to listen to every lecture twice?

Given the particular circumstance in which the tape recorder may be of help, developing an effective system of note taking is a far more useful procedure than tape-recording lectures.

A System for Note Taking[2]

Phase 1: Before the Lecture

1 Select a looseleaf notebook with 8½- by 11-inch paper, the standard large-size looseleaf notebook.

2 Draw a vertical line 2½ inches from the left side of each sheet and a horizontal line 2 inches from the bottom, as illustrated in Figure 2-1.

3 Review notes in previous lectures to provide continuity.

Phase 2: During the Lecture

1 Record notes on the right-hand side of the paper. Try to capture the main points of the lecture. Do not be concerned with developing an elabo-

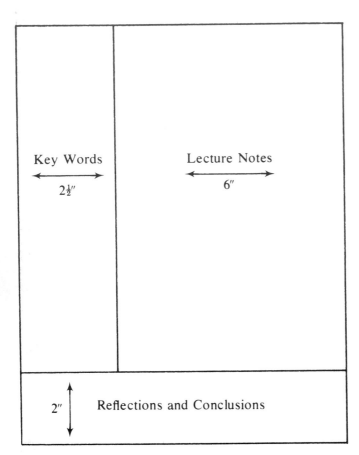

Figure 2-1
Preparing your looseleaf notebook for note taking.

rate formal outline using roman numerals, capital letters, and the like. Subtopics under main points can be indicated with numbers or simply with a dash placed in front of each subtopic. Or you can do the following:

List main points at the left margin.

Indent the secondary points and supporting material.

Indent additional subordinate material even more.

2 Write so that you will be able to read the material. This may mean practicing a form of printing. It may also mean developing a system of abbreviations. But be careful when using abbreviations to use only those you are quite familiar with. Common abbreviations include the following:

And	&
With	w/
Without	w/o
For example	e.g.
Example	ex.
Definition	def.
Therefore	∴
Equal	=
Does not equal	≠

You will become much more efficient if you can learn to write your lecture notes both legibly enough and completely enough so that you don't have to type them after each lecture. Though your notes will obviously be neater if you type them, most students do not have the extra time required for typing.

Phase 3: After the Lecture

1 As soon as possible after the lecture, jot down key words and phrases from the lecture on the left side of the paper. Not only does this procedure help you to recall the lecture, but also the process of writing summarizing words and phrases helps to fix the information in your mind.

2 Cover the right side of the notebook page so that you are looking only at the key words and phrases. Try to restate the lecture in your own words from these key cues. Uncover the notes, then verify the accuracy of your work.

3 Reflect on the meaning of the lecture. Can you think of examples from your experience or from your reading to illustrate main points? Perhaps you arrive at a conclusion that is different from the lecturer's. You may discover that the lecture raised several questions you want to pursue further. On the bottom of your notebook page, in the section reserved for reflections and questions, jot down your thoughts and questions. This can be the most important part of the entire process of listening to a lecture and taking notes, for it is during the reflection step that you are integrating the new information. You are relating the new information to what you already know and are trying to give the information meaning for yourself. As we pointed out earlier, learning is much more than memorizing what the lecturer says or what is written in a book or a journal. It fundamentally involves giving information meaning for yourself.

4 Occasionally review your notes. As mentioned above, review the previous lecture's notes before attending the next lecture. Occasionally during the semester review all your lecture notes. One way to do this is to cover the right side of the notes and see if you can recall the content of the lecture. Meeting with other students in the course is another profitable way to review your notes. Not only can you review the main points with each other, but you may also discover that other students have heard points you haven't. Perhaps they saw the relationship of points to each other differently than you did. Input from other students can be one more source of information for you as you try to give meaning to what you are studying.

Note-Taking Exercise Prepare a sheet of notepaper as suggested above. Then ask a friend to read the following as if it were a class lecture. Ask your friend to read slowly and clearly while you listen and take notes. Don't read the lecture yourself. This "lecture" is much shorter than most lectures; but the principles of note-taking are the same, no matter what length the lecture.

Today our topic is problems. What is so complicated about problems, you ask? We all have them and we all know about them. We have problems balancing our family budgets. We sometimes have problems with our children. Some of us may have problems with our health. We may have problems with our car, and so on. Our lives are made up of one problem after the other it seems. But what do we really know about problems? Just exactly what is a problem, fundamentally?

For our purposes today, I define a problem as a question raised for inquiry, for solution, or for both. Let me write that on the board. Problem: question raised for inquiry, for solution, or for both.

Let's look at that definition a moment. First, problems are questions. Second, problems are questions that may be raised for either inquiry or for a solution. That is, we may choose to study a problem, inquire about it, without attempting to solve it. And third, problems are questions that are raised for both inquiry and for solution. We study the problem and we attempt to solve it as well.

Let's look at some examples. Take for instance the problem of world trade imbalance—more U.S. dollars leaving the country than other countries' money coming in. Following our definition of problem, to say simply "world trade imbalance" is not to state a problem. We must turn it into a question. We could ask, Why does the United States suffer from a trade imbalance? Or, Which countries contribute to our trade imbalance? We could also ask, What can we do to correct the trade imbalance?

At another level, we could ask, Why does my car get such poor gas mileage? All of these are problem questions. We could study the question of why the United States suffers from trade imbalance and learn considerably about the problem—but do nothing to solve it. We could likewise learn why our car delivers such poor gas mileage and do nothing about it. Thus it is possible to study a problem, inquire about it, without attempting to solve it. It is also possible to seek a solution to a problem without studying the problem at all. We could purchase some additive for our gasoline tank that is supposed to ensure us greater gas mileage without ever thinking about why our car delivers poor gas mileage.

Of course we could do both, that is, both study a problem and attempt to solve it. Now, what we have said so far is this: We have said problems are questions. Secondly, we have said problems may be raised for either inquiry or for solution; or they may be raised for both inquiry and solution.

Now let's go on. Let's attempt to answer the question, Are all problems solvable? Many would answer, "Of course all problems are solvable. It may take time and money and expertise, but eventually all problems can be solved."

My position is that not all problems can be solved. So we end up with solvable and insolvable problems. Let's look at the characteristics of each. First, solvable problems.

When people begin to work on a solvable problem, take it apart, look at its pieces, and search out information about it, they find that the more they work on the problem the more they see the answers they are finding come together. All paths begin leading to the same destination—the solution to the problem.

Basically we have two types of solvable problems: First, those that can be solved immediately or in the near future, and secondly, those that we know have the potential for being solved but we may not yet have the technology or the resources for solving them. An example of the first type is a home computer that will figure one's income tax. An example of the second type, a solvable problem that is not yet solved is space travel—the problem is potentially solvable, but it is not yet solved.

Now let's turn to insolvable problems. When we attempt to answer an insolvable problem, we discover the answers leading away from each other rather than toward each other. In fact we may find two answers to the problem that both sound plausible, but they contradict each other. For instance let's look at the question, How do people learn? If we examine that question we discover several points of view. Some claim people learn best by starting with pieces and adding them together to make wholes. Others believe we start with the whole, and then deal with the pieces. Though they are totally opposed to each other, each of these answers is plausible. So the problem of how do people learn is insolvable.

We have, then, solvable and insolvable problems. Next time we'll begin discussing the relationship between these two types of problems.

Now go over your notes as suggested in "Phase 3: After the Lecture." Jot down the key words on the left side of the note page. Try to recall the lecture from the key words. Then, write down your reaction to the lecture, or questions that remain unanswered for you. Following is a sample set of notes taken from this lecture. No two sets of notes will be alike. But your notes should contain the main points listed here.

Example Lecture Notes

Management 112
Problems
  Family budget
  Car
*Def. Problem: Question raised for inquiry, for solution or both (Bd.)
  1 Problems are questions
  2 Questions for inquiry *or* solution
  3 Questions for inquiry *and* solution
  Ex.
  1 Trade imbalance—why? Which countries contribute? What to do?
  2 Car—poor mileage
  Alternatives: Study problem without solving
                Solve problem without study
                Study and solve problems
 All problems solvable?
  Many say yes
  Prof says no
  Solvable problem—answers come together
  1 Solve now—income tax on the home computer (Ex.)
  2 Solve soon—space travel (Ex.)
  Insolvable problems—answers go apart
  Ex. How people learn
    1 Parts to whole?
    2 Whole to parts?
 Next time:
  Relationship: Solvable and insolvable problems

Listening

"Listening—I don't have any problems with that," is what you are probably saying. We all think we can listen, yet many of us have problems doing it. The tendency is to hear what we want to hear or hear that with which we are familiar.

Listening is an integral part of all the learning opportunities described above. The possible exception is independent study, although now many independent-study units include cassette tapes as part of the independent-study package. Some of the learning opportunities, such as the lecture, depend heavily on the student's ability to listen.

Blocks to listening   What are some of the reasons why we don't listen well? You already know most of them. If you are not interested in what a speaker has to say, you don't listen well. You may, for instance, be enrolled in a statistics course. You are not interested in the subject; you would never have selected the course had you a choice. Yet you are enrolled in it because it is a requirement of the program in which you are enrolled. Your attitude toward the subject can get in the way of your listening.

Likewise, if you dislike the instructor in your course, this dislike can block your listening. This is particularly a problem if the instructor is teaching a lecture course, in which he or she speaks to you and probably 200 or 300 others for 50 minutes each Monday, Wednesday, and Friday.

The teacher's mannerisms—she tugs on her left ear; he says "you know" five times in 5 minutes—may distract you from listening. You have all heard about college students who spend their time during lectures counting the number of times in 50 minutes the professor says "and ah."

Inability to concentrate is a problem for many returning students and often is a serious block to listening. Letting your mind wander to personal problems, other assignments, your job, or a hundred other things will prevent you from listening. If concentration is a problem for you, a simple technique is to make a check mark on your note page every time you catch yourself not concentrating on what is being said. You may initially have twenty or more check marks on a page, but after doing this for a week or two you should be able to reduce the number to one or two.[3]

Distractions such as a room that is too warm, interesting events outside the classroom window, and an air hammer working in the street are all obvious blocks to listening.

Loss of ability to hear is a block to listening. As we pointed out earlier, a natural occurrence for all of us as we grow older is to experience some hearing loss. This is usually easily corrected, of course.

Improving Listening   Given the potential blocks, what can you do to improve your listening skills? Let's assume that any problem of hearing loss has been corrected.

Become an Active Listener   Later we'll discuss how to become an active reader. Many of the same principles apply to listening. In fact there are many similarities between the processes of speaking and writing.

Both the speaker and the writer are concerned with explaining, convincing, entertaining, or some combination of the three.

Both the speaker and the writer, if they are effective, have an organization to what they are saying or writing; that is, there is a beginning, a middle, and an end to the lecture or speech, and there is a beginning, a middle, and an end to the article or book.

There are also obvious differences between speaking and writing. In a lecture, communication includes more than the words the instructor is speaking. The way the lecturer stands, the gestures made, the tone of voice, the increasing and decreasing of voice volume as words and sentences are spoken, the eye contact made with the group are all clues that if understood can help you get more from the lectures. This nonverbal communication is an extremely important part of speaking. We must be able to ''hear'' with our eyes as well as with our ears when we are attending a lecture.

When reading you of course don't have the advantage of the extra communication provided by nonverbal clues, but you are able to read a passage you don't understand several times. Of course when listening to a lecture you hear it once—unless you use a tape recorder to record the lecture. Not only do you hear what the lecturer has to say only once; also you must listen at the rate at which the lecturer speaks. Most of us are able to listen considerably faster than the average speaking speed. All of us with average reading ability are able to read faster than someone speaks.

An advantage of being able to listen and think faster than a lecturer speaks is the ability to relate what the lecturer is saying to what has been said previously and perhaps to reading you've done or an experience you've had. A disadvantage is that you often find your mind wandering to other topics: what you should prepare for dinner, how nice it would be on the golf course, and what's happening at work while you are away.

Be prepared   Read the assignments and the previous notes you've taken before coming to the lecture so that you can put into context the new material you will be receiving.

Raise Questions while You Listen   You usually have time while listening to wrestle with the material you are hearing, not to just soak it up like a sponge. Typical questions you might ask yourself include: What support does she have for that statement? How does he justify that in light of professor X's research on the same topic? How does she explain the apparent contradiction between what she said today and what she said Monday? What is the relationship of point 1 to point 2?

At another level you could ask: Why can't I make sense out of what he is saying? Does what she is saying make sense to anyone in this room?

Learn the Lecturing Style of the Professor   Most students become quite adept at figuring out their professors. There is nothing wrong with this, particularly if it helps their learning. Some professors begin lecturers by giving a short outline of what they plan to cover that day. Others very carefully summarize what they have said at the end of their lectures. Many use the chalkboard or other visual devices to outline the main points they make in their lectures. Some use such verbal devices as "My first point is . . ." and "There are four important concepts in this theory." Some present a major idea and then give a careful description and explanation employing many illustrations and examples. Occasionally a lecturer provides a written outline of the lecture or a brief summary of the important points covered. Many lecturers repeat important ideas. All these clues, once learned for a particular instructor, can be important tools for increasing listening.

Keep Notes while You Listen   Of all the suggestions this is likely the most important, for not only does it aid your listening, but also it provides you with a record of the main points of the lecture. Note taking aids listening because it forces you to pay attention to what is being said and to try and make sense out of it so that you can record the main points.

Listening in a Group   Several of the learning opportunities described above are based on group discussion, on participants speaking as well as listening. Some students have problems in listening in such group situations. Many students are so highly motivated to participate, to talk, that they forget that group discussion involves listening as well. What happens is that they spend most or all their time thinking about what to say and little or no time listening to what others are saying. What happens in these discussions—and they occur outside of academic situations as well as within them—is that people talk past each other. Outside observers describe these discussions as a series of minispeeches with no real discussion taking place.

A good group discussion leader can help correct this situation by insisting on better listening. One technique is to insist that a person responding to another person first summarize what the other person has said before making a new point.

In many ways listening in a group discussion setting is more difficult than listening in a lecture situation. The organization of discussion is almost always much looser than a lecture, even to the point of total disorganization in some discussions. And students have the dual responsibility of speaking and listening. Some students end up speaking during the entire discussion without ever listening; others spend all their time trying to listen and thinking of something to say. They end up totally frustrated because they haven't been able to listen well and they never got a chance to say anything either.

One general suggestion for group discussion participants is to relax. Listen carefully, respond when you have something to say, and don't worry that you are speaking more or less than someone else in the group.

Listening Exercise[4] The following exercise is one that can help you improve your listening ability or at least help you determine if you have any listening problems. It requires that you convince two friends to work with you.

1 Number yourselves 1, 2, and 3.
2 Each person selects a topic to discuss. Something that is controversial often adds to the interest. Topics might include:
  a Women should be allowed in combat as well as in other military occupations.
  b All oil production in the United States should be taken over by the federal government because the resource is limited.
  c Automobiles should be banned from the downtown sections of all cities of over 100,000 population.
3 For an agreed-upon time, say, 5 minutes, persons 1 and 2 discuss a topic person 1 selects. Person 1 is the speaker and person 2, the listener. Before speaker 2 can comment on anything that speaker 1 says, he or she must summarize what speaker 1 has said. If the summary is thought incorrect, the speaker or the referee (3) is free to interrupt and clear up the problem.
4 After 5 minutes of discussion between the speaker and the listener, person 2 becomes the speaker, person 3 the listener, and person 1 the referee. The new speaker chooses a topic, and the discussion continues. This procedure continues until all three have been speaker, listener, and referee.
5 When all three have had an opportunity to play the three roles, the group can discuss such questions as:
  a Did you have trouble listening and thinking about what to say at the same time?
  b Did you spend time rehearsing in your mind what you were going to say?
  c Did you ever forget what you were going to say?

d Did you have trouble saying what you wanted to say?

e What listening problem(s) did this exercise point up for you?

To become a better listener:

Be prepared: read assignments and previous notes
Raise questions while you listen
Learn lecturing style of professor
Take notes while you listen
Judge content, not delivery
Resist distractions
Concentrate on listening

Taking Examinations

Fear of tests   Of all the activities associated with returning to school, taking tests produces the most anxiety for the adult student. One of the students who answered the survey on problems adults faced when returning to school wrote:

> I am very uptight about exams. I hate multiple-choice tests because they are usually tricky. They don't test anything more than the professor's ability to write tricky exams. I feel insulted taking such tests. I am more comfortable with short-answer or essay questions if they are pertinent to the scope of the course. True-false questions are ok if one has the opportunity to justify the answer. I prefer writing a term paper or talking with the professor in an informal way in lieu of taking exams.

Another returning student wrote: "One major difficulty I encountered when I returned to school was readjusting to exam taking. I found objective examinations particularly frustrating. They didn't measure my learning well."

These are brief samples of the many complaints and fears of adults who are faced with taking examinations. The fears are certainly understandable. In many ways adults are putting their futures on the line when they return to school, and many of them believe they are putting their personal worth on the line too. Being successful in school is of prime importance, indeed is a necessity, to them.

The examination is viewed as the instrument that will determine their success; it is the measure of how well they are doing. Exams are used heavily by many institutions of higher education as the sole determinant of how well the student is meeting the requirements of a course.

This extreme emphasis on examinations, which is still present in many courses, indeed contributes to fear of taking tests.

Even though examinations may be overemphasized in some instances, they are still one useful way for you to determine what progress you are making in your learning as well as for the instructor to determine how well you are meeting course requirements.

Building Confidence in Taking Tests   Taking tests is not just part of formal education. Tests are part of our modern-day life. To obtain a driver's license you must take a test. To apply for a civil service job you must take a test. When you are interviewed for a job you are taking an oral examination. When you fill out vocabulary quizzes in popular magazines you are taking tests. When you complete one of the many self-assessment questionnaires in popular magazines and newspapers, such as "What is Your Love-making Quotient?" or "What Type of Leader Are You?" you are taking an examination.

All adults face many examinations as they live their lives. Those who run for office, say, for a position on the school board, are examined through forums, interviews, speeches, and the like. Persons who are involved in helping to solve community problems face many examinations, even though these situations are not called examinations. They are questioned (examined) about the problem they are trying to solve and the solutions they are suggesting.

These types of examinations, which all of us face constantly, are much more subtle and in most cases have much more far-reaching effects than an examination taken as part of a college course.

What we must do, then, is to realize that examinations are part of life, for they are without question. Then we must put the examinations we face as part of a course into perspective along with all the other examinations we have faced and will face in life. As we reflect on how we have handled other examination situations—usually quite successfully—we can face a course examination with considerable confidence.

On the practical side, an occasional complaint from both more traditional students and returning adult students is not knowing how they are doing. Tests of course are one input to answering the question, How am I doing? This is especially true if you are studying in an area that is new to you and you have little basis upon which to judge the effectiveness of your study efforts. If you can see the value of taking an examination, you are more likely to come to the experience with a positive attitude.

Another way to build your confidence in taking tests is to develop some skills for doing it. The remainder of this chapter focuses on helping you increase your test-taking skills. You are also encouraged to explore the topic further by referring to the readings suggested at the end of the chapter.

Types of Tests   In a broad sense there are two types of tests, achievement and aptitude. Achievement tests measure what you have learned; aptitude tests measure your potential to do something. Our focus here will be only on achievement tests. But if you are faced with taking an aptitude test, be sure to study suggestions for taking such tests. Some readings with instructions and sample test questions are included in the list at the end of the chapter. Often you will be able to find specific suggestions for taking the particular kind of aptitude test you face.

Achievement tests are of two types, commonly referred to as (1) *essay* and (2) *objective*. Essay tests include those requiring short answers and those asking for an extended discussion. Objective tests include true-false, multiple-choice, fill-in-the-blanks, and matching tests. None of these types of tests is new to you. You've likely been exposed to them in one way or another since you attended elementary school.

We can also look at tests according to their form. You are all familiar with the written examination taken in the classroom setting. Other forms are the open-book examination, which is growing in popularity, and the oral examination, in which the student meets with his or her instructor to answer questions orally. Proponents of the open-book examination argue that this is the most realistic form of testing. In life, you are most apt to face situations in which you have a paper to write or a speech to give, and you will make use of resources you have available to you.

Preparing for Exams   Here are some general principles useful in preparing for an examination, no matter if it is an essay or an objective type:

1 Practice continuous reading and review. Preparing for an examination begins when you begin a course. If you keep up with the reading, keep good notes that you review occasionally, and spend time reflecting on the meaning of what you are studying, you are preparing for any examination. Part of this reflection process is focusing on the course in total. What is the big picture? How do the parts of that picture, the topics in the course, relate to each other and to the total picture?

Studying for a mathematics examination requires some special techniques in addition to those suggested here. Refer to these readings for math help:

Brown, Gary E.: *A Student's Guide to Academic Survival,* Harper & Row, New York, 1973.

Davis, Robert D. and Robert G. Moon: *Elementary Algebra,* 2d ed., Merrill, Columbus, Ohio, 1970.

Ehrlich, Eugene H.: *How to Study Better and Get Better Marks,* Crowell, New York, 1961.

Geiselmann, Harrison: "How to Study Mathematics," in Walter Pauk, *How to Study in College,* 2d ed., Houghton Mifflin, Boston, 1974, pp. 221–235.

Tobias, Sheila: *Overcoming Math Anxiety,* Houghton Mifflin, Boston, 1978.

2 A systematic review a week or so prior to an examination can be most helpful. This is not the same as cramming, in which you try to do several weeks worth of reading and study in a few concentrated hours. Systematic review includes going over lecture notes and, if possible, meeting with other students to discuss what you are learning. Do not depend on other students, though, to tell you what you need to know for the examination. Systematic study includes both individual effort and group work with other students. When meeting with other students you can clear up areas in which you are unsure, try out your conclusions, and ask each other typical examination questions. Often textbooks include review questions at the end of chapters, and sometimes instructors distribute review questions to students.

3 Do not alter your regular life schedule. Some students advocate cramming all night prior to an examination and keeping awake with coffee or something stronger. A schedule of eating, sleeping, recreation, etc., should help you to be mentally alert for an exam and will usually be of more benefit to you than extended hours of studying prior to an examination.

4 Relax.

5 If previous examinations in the course are available, it is helpful to look at them. You can get an idea of the type of questions the instructor asks—essay or objective—and you can see what content areas were stressed previously.

6 Try to guess what questions may appear on the exam, and prepare answers for them.

Taking Exams   Below are suggestions students have found helpful for taking examinations, no matter what the type. Later we'll share specific suggestions for taking objective and essay exams.

1 Arrive at the examination room a little ahead of time so that you can find a comfortable chair and can relax. Avoid getting into conversations with students about specific topics in the course. Make sure you have with you pencils, erasers, and whatever other aids are allowed, such as a calculator.

2 Listen carefully to any oral instructions for taking the examination, and read the examination instructions carefully. If any instruction is unclear, ask for clarification. Many students skip over the instructions quickly in their haste to begin the examination, and often they miss some important instructions.

The instructions will often tell you the point value for the questions, whether you need to answer all the questions or have a choice, the type of answer required (in a math test you are often required to show your calculations as well as the answer), and whether or not you must follow a particular order in answering the questions.

Below is an exercise to test your direction-following ability.

CAN-YOU-FOLLOW-DIRECTIONS EXERCISE*

Read these directions carefully. You have 3 minutes to complete the exercise. Ask a friend to time you. Be sure to write legibly. When you have finished, check your answers against the directions. Read carefully all the following directions before beginning.

1 On a sheet of 8½- by 11-inch paper, print your name in the upper right-hand corner, last name first.
2 Make ten X's in the upper left-hand corner of the paper. Begin with a capital X, and alternate lower-case and capital X's.
3 Write the numerals 10 to 0 backwards down the right-hand side of the page, beginning just under your last name.
4 Draw a big heart at the bottom left-hand corner of your paper. Shade it in heavily with your pencil.
5 Draw a tic tac toe board in the lower right-hand corner of your paper.
6 Add 42 and 56. Divide that sum by 49. Draw that many triangles in the center of the page.
7 Now that you have read all the directions, simply do number 1 and turn over your paper.

*Adapted from "Test," used by Counseling Services, University of Wisconsin-Madison.

---

3 Plan your time for the exam. Look over the entire test and set up a time budget. Allot the most time for the questions that give you the most points.

4 Start to answer the questions immediately.

5 First answer the questions you know well, then go back and work on other questions.

6 Read every word in the test questions. You may read into a question something that isn't there if you don't read it carefully.

7 Attempt to answer all the questions even if you are not absolutely certain of the answers.

8 Check your answers for obvious errors before turning in the exam paper.

Answering Essay Questions   Essay examinations are designed to measure whether you know the answers to the questions, but they also measure your ability to organize and present ideas clearly. Here are some suggestions that many students have found helpful in completing essay exams:

1 Carefully budget your time, saving time at the end for editing.

2 Read all the essay questions before beginning to write on any of them. Occasionally questions are related to each other. Certain questions are usually given more test points than others.

3 As you read the questions, jot down alongside each question words that come to mind for answering the question. Doing this will alleviate any fears you may have about forgetting important points.

4 Read the key words in each question so that you know exactly what you are required to do. Some frequent key words and their meanings are as follows:

Define   Write a concise, clear, authoritative meaning. Write what clearly differentiates what you are defining from everything else.

Compare   Examine qualities or characteristics to show resemblances. Emphasize similarities between the things you are asked to compare.

Contrast   Stress differences or unlikenesses between the things you are asked to contrast.

List   Provide an itemized series or a tabulation.

Outline   Develop an organized description. Give main points and essential supplementary material.

Analyze   Show the nature of the parts and the relationship of the parts to each other and to the whole.

Explain   State the how and why. Reconcile any differences in opinion or experimental results. Where possible state causes.

5 Develop a brief outline for your answer before beginning to write. This will help you be concise and yet not leave out important information.

6 Write those answers that you know best first.

7 Write concisely to the question. Answer the question directly, then support your answer. Avoid bringing in information that is only remotely related to the question. Feel free to quote authorities to support your answer, but not to take the place of *your* answer.

8 Write legibly.

9 Unless asked especially to do something different, such as develop a list or an outline, write your responses to essay questions in complete sentences and in paragraph form.

10 Leave some space after each answer to add additional information that may later come to mind.

11 Read through your answer, correcting obvious errors in spelling and punctuation, and make sure the answer says what you intended to say.

12 If you run out of time, outline the answers to remaining questions rather than leaving them blank or partially answered in narrative form.

Writing Objective Examinations While essay questions measure your ability to organize and present ideas clearly, objective test questions focus primarily on your ability to recall and relate specific information:

1 After reading the specific directions for the examination, survey the entire examination to note the number of questions and the point values in relation to the time you have for the examination.

2 If the examination answers are marked on a separate answer sheet, make sure while taking the examination to check occasionally that the answer number corresponds with the test question number.

3 Go through the questions quickly, answering those that you are sure about. Then work through again, spending more time, if necessary, on the difficult questions.

4 Answer every question, even those you are not absolutely sure about.

5 Pay attention to key words in the examination questions. Statements containing the modifiers *all, always,* or *never* tend to be false. Statements containing the words *usually, most, some,* or *may* tend to be true.

6 Use logical reasoning in attempting to answer questions. If the response to a multiple-choice is unclear to you, by elimination cross off those responses that you know are incorrect. You may end up with one response left, which must be the correct answer, or you may have two responses from which you must select, an easier task than selecting from five.

7 Look for information in test questions that may help you answer other questions.

8 Read back through your exam when it is completed for any obvious errors you may have made. But be careful about changing responses to questions you answered and weren't sure about. Often the first response to such questions is the best response.

Writing Open-Book Examinations A growing number of instructors recognize that real life situations often require a person to use available resources when attempting to resolve a problem or answer a question. Many of these instructors give open-book exams to their students. Some open-book exams are written in class, while others are take-home exams with deadlines of a week or more for completion.

An open-book examination, like an essay examination, measures the student's ability to organize and present ideas. It also measures the student's ability to find and organize the information necessary to answer the questions. The following tips may be useful for those faced with writing an open-book examination:

1 Preparation is extremely important. Do not procrastinate, with the false security that you will be able to go to resources for the answers. You will not have time to do the necessary reading while you are answering the exam, so this reading must be done ahead of time. Preparing for an open-book examination is thus no different from preparing for an essay or an objective examination. You must review your lecture notes and your reading notes before the exam. And you must do considerable thinking about the meaning of what you have been studying, about how the pieces all fit together.

2 Find the books, articles, and notes that you anticipate will be useful for the exam.

3 Organize the material you are studying into broad topics. These are usually stated in the course outline, or syllabus. Then indicate pages from your readings which apply to each of the topics. Key your lecture notes to the main topics in the same fashion.

4 Anticipate the questions that may be asked, and outline how you would respond to the questions, referring to readings and lecture notes as required.

5 When you actually receive the examination, spend some time organizing your answers and keying to potential readings where you might find assistance. Do not be in a hurry to begin writing. If you have 5 days for the exam, 2 days of thinking about the questions and organizing the answers is not too long.

6 Make sure your answers to the questions are concise and to the point. Do not string together a series of quotations from various sources with the idea that doing this constitutes giving an appropriate answer to the question. Write the answers in your own words, using support in the form of an occasional quotation or reference to resource materials.

7 For open-book take-home examinations type your answers if at all possible. Usually you can plan your time so that you not only have time to read through and edit your answers, but you also have time to type them. Most instructors appreciate typewritten copy for ease in reading the material.

When the Results Are in   Without question, examinations, whatever form they take, can be useful learning experiences. When you get back your written examination—and you should insist on seeing your corrected examination—study it to see where you made mistakes. This perusal should give you clues as to where you need to go back and reread or to do additional work in a given area.

Many instructors will spend time in class reviewing an examination to explain the answers to the questions. This of course can be extremely useful.

Taking Oral Examinations   Some instructors give oral examinations. These are more common at the graduate level than at the undergraduate level. The oral examination measures your ability to analyze and integrate material and to organize it quickly into a verbal response to a question.

Students have found the following tips helpful when taking oral examinations:

1 Before the exam know what the scope will be. Will the entire course be covered, or only part of it?

2 Rehearse the exam. Anticipate the questions that may be asked, and practice answering them. This procedure works best when done with another student taking the same exam.

3 Listen carefully to the question as it is asked. If you don't completely understand a question, ask the instructor for clarification.

4 Don't bluff. If you don't know the answer, say so. But don't hesitate to attempt an answer that you are not sure of. You may know more than you think.

5 After you are asked a question, take time to think through and organize your response.

6 Usually you can get immediate feedback from an oral examination. When it is over, ask for clarification in areas where you weren't sure. Often, when you finish your response to a question, the instructor will immediately comment on what you've said, may ask you a related question, or may share with you the answer he or she intended for the question.

SUMMARY

This chapter focused on three skills that will help you as a returning student—listening, taking notes, and preparing and taking examinations.

All students have available to them many learning opportunities: the traditional lecture, lecture-discussion, discussion, seminar, laboratory, informal discussion, independent study both guided and self-planned, and internship.

Basic study skills, such as reading, writing, thinking, listening, taking notes, and taking examinations, are required to make the most of these learning opportunities. Succeeding chapters in the book will cover reading, writing, and thinking.

Removal of blocks to listening, such as attitude toward the speaker and the subject, will improve your listening ability. Some tips for increasing listening skills include the following: (1) become an active listener, (2) raise questions while you listen, (3) learn the lecturing style of the professor, and (4) keep notes while you listen.

Listening in a group discussion presents a special set of problems. Many persons are so intent on thinking about what they are going to say that they don't hear what is being said.

One system for note taking includes using paper marked with space for recording notes, key words, and personal reflections and conclusions. The key words and personal reflections are written after the lecture.

Taking tests unfortunately is seen by many returning students as one of the most difficult and anxiety-laden tasks associated with returning to school. Yet after some thought, one quickly realizes that examinations in one form or another are taken throughout life, more often outside of formal educational settings than within them. There should be no real reason to become more anxious about a formal examination than about many of the informal examinations to which we are all subjected.

Several suggestions are offered on how to take essay, objective, open-book, and oral examinations. For all these examinations, continuous review and study of the material included in the course is the best preparation for the examination and the best way to allay unreasonable fears.

REFERENCES

1 Allen Tough, *The Adult's Learning Projects,* The Ontario Institute for Studies in Education, Research in Education Series no. 1, Toronto, Ontario, 1971, p. 1.

2 Refer to Walter Pauk, *How to Study in College,* 2d ed., Houghton Mifflin, Boston, 1974, pp. 125–139, and Clifford T. Morgan and James Deese, *How to Study,* McGraw-Hill, New York, 1969, pp. 29–32, for additional information on this topic.

3 For a more in-depth discussion on this topic refer to Pauk, op. cit., pp. 35–51.

4 Adapted from J. William Pfeiffer and John E. Jones, *A Handbook of Structured Experiences for Human Relations Training,* University Associates Press, Iowa City, Iowa, 1969, pp. 31–34.

BOOKS WITH SAMPLE EXAMINATION QUESTIONS

Cash, Phyllis, *How to Prepare for the Miller Analogies Test,* McGraw-Hill, New York, 1979.

Evarts, Prescott, Jr., *How to Prepare for the American College Testing Program (ACT),* McGraw-Hill, New York, 1980.

———, *How to Prepare for the College Level Examination Program (CLEP),* McGraw-Hill, New York, 1980.

Goodman, Roger, *How to Prepare for the Graduate Record Examination—Verbal Section,* McGraw-Hill, New York, 1979.

Gruber, Gary, *Preparation for the Scholastic Aptitude Test (SAT),* Contemporary Books, Chicago, 1978.

Israel, Benjamin, *How to Prepare for the Professional and Administrative Career Examination,* McGraw-Hill, New York, 1980.

CHAPTER 3

IMPROVE YOUR READING ABILITY

"I wanted to read each book from cover to cover, as I had done at home for the past 14 years."

"Reading for content—identifying key concepts and ideas—was particularly a problem for me."

"I found the reading material more difficult than in previous courses I'd taken."

"The most difficult problem I faced was adjusting to a social science emphasis, having come from the physical sciences. This adjustment was most pressing in regard to the reading skills I had previously acquired. Instead of reading for specific details and terminologies, the subject required, in the education courses in which I enrolled, concentrating on broader concepts and extracting the essence of material from the readings."

"When I returned to school, the main problem I had was in the area of reading. My reading is slow, and I had difficulty in allocating my time among the reading assignments for the courses I was taking."

These are comments made by returning students that point up the problems they faced with reading.

This chapter is designed to help solve the problems represented in these statements. In the first section seven principles for improving reading are presented. The remainder of the chapter focuses on how to improve your reading skills when reading for information, for understanding, to criticize, and to create.

Though this chapter is directed toward the returning student, it also has broader application. No matter what your position in life, reading is part of it. Some people would have us believe that our society is moving away from reading to a television-type mentality in which everything is pictures and sound. The evidence denies this. One need only inspect the sales of books each year to learn of our society's great thirst for the written word.

There are many audiovisual opportunities available to students today. Nevertheless, the printed word continues to be foundational to all formal education.

GENERAL PRINCIPLES FOR IMPROVING READING

1 Read with a Purpose

One of the most common errors made by students, and by other readers as well, is that they read all material the same way. They assume that there is only one purpose for reading. Later in this chapter I will discuss four purposes for reading: to get information, to understand, to criticize, and to create. A reader must first decide what the purpose is when reading any material. How the material is read, as we shall see later, depends on the purpose for doing the reading.

2 Determine the Type and Quality of the Material

Reading is often classified into several broad areas: fiction, nonfiction, poetry, and plays. Nonfiction can be further broken into such areas as articles, empirical research reports, essays, and textbooks. Some people classify nonfiction into theoretical and practical. Of course nonfiction writing may also be classified according to broad subject fields such as history, science, and philosophy.

The point is not to quibble about classification systems, but to emphasize that one reads a novel differently from the way one reads an essay. The fiction writer communicates a message to the reader through description and the development of a story plot. The essay writer, on the other hand, is far less subtle. In a logical, straightforward manner the essayist presents a position on a question or issue and then argues that it is the correct position. The textbook writer, also in a logical, well-organized fashion, presents information on a topic, usually in as objective a manner as possible. The textbook writer usually does not argue for a given position, as does the essay writer.

Knowing ahead of time what type of material you are reading gives you some clues about how to read it. If you are reading an essay, you know that only one point of view is being presented. If you are reading a novel, you don't search for specific information organized in a systematic fashion. An excellent reference that describes in some depth how to read various kinds of writing is *How to Read a Book,* by Mortimer J. Adler and Charles Van Doren.[1]

Determining the quality of a book or other reading material is sometimes not an easy task for the person who is reading in a relatively new area. Later in this chapter, when we discuss how to criticize writing, several suggestions are offered to help you determine the quality of material you are reading. When you become acquainted with a given area of writing, you will be able to quite quickly determine the quality of a given piece of writing in the area. Material of low quality obviously should take less of your time than that which is of higher quality. Francis Bacon said it well when he wrote, ''Some books are to be tasted, others to be swallowed, and some few to be chewed and digested; that is some books are to be read only in parts . . . and some few to be read wholly, and with diligence and attention.''[2]

3   Adjust Reading Speed to Purpose and Type of Material

Speed-reading courses have been and continue to be popular. Some of them advertise that participants are able to increase the rate of their reading well beyond 1000 words a minute with high comprehension rates.

It is likely true that most of us can and probably should read faster than we do. But the important point to note is that not all reading material should be read quickly. Some of it should be read very slowly. To attempt to read a statistics book and comprehend the concepts by speed reading is absurd. The same goes for almost any science or mathematics book or any empirical research report or a carefully drawn philosophical argument.

Some materials may be read rapidly and then later read more carefully once the overall ideas of the book or article are determined. Depending on the purpose, some materials may be read rapidly to provide you with information you are seeking. There is no reason for reading them slowly and carefully.

Thus rapid reading depends on (1) the type of material you are reading and (2) the purpose for which you are reading it.

Some people are not aware of their reading rate, nor are they aware of the rates that are considered ''good'' depending on the type of material they are reading.

Raygor and Schick suggest the following as guidelines:

When reading recreationally, a light novel, a short story, or an article in such popular magazines as *Reader's Digest,* one's reading rate should be 500 words per minute and up.

When reading fiction with some focus on the characterization and when reading nonfiction to find the main ideas, an adequate reading rate is 350 to 500 words per minute.

When reading complex fiction with the intent of analyzing the plot or determining more subtle elements of characterization, or when reading nonfiction to note details or to determine the relationships among ideas, a reading rate of 250 to 350 per minute is suggested.

When reading highly technical material, when attempting to criticize the merit of what you are reading, or when reading to solve a problem or follow directions, a reading rate as slow as 100 to 250 words per minute is appropriate.[3]

How to Determine Your Reading Speed

a Select a chapter in a book or an article in a journal or magazine.

b Determine what type of reading it is and what your purpose is for reading it.

c Count the number of words in the chapter or article. (Count the number of words in ten lines. Divide by 10 to determine the average number of words per line. Count the number of lines in the chapter or article and multiply by number of words per line.)

d Read the chapter or article, noting beginning time and ending time in minutes and seconds.

e Divide total number of words by time to determine words per minute.

f Compare your rate with standards suggested above for the type of reading and your purpose.

Most of us can read much of the material we read faster than we do. But the key is not reading faster, but learning when to read fast and when to read more slowly and deliberately. When we are reading material that does not demand complete and careful attention, we should push ourselves to move through it quickly. But when we are faced, for example, with writing a critical book review, we should read much more slowly and deliberately.

Select a chapter in a book or an article and complete the following form to determine your reading speed.

1 Material read: _____

2 Number of words in ten lines: _____

3 Words per line $= \dfrac{\text{Words in ten lines}}{10} =$ _____

4 Number of lines in chapter or article: _____

5 Number of words = words per line × number of lines = _____

6 Beginning reading time: _____
7 Ending reading time: _____
8 Total reading time: _____

9 Reading speed per minute $= \dfrac{\text{Total words (line 5)}}{\text{Total reading time}} =$ _____ words

per minute

Example:

1 Material read: _____ Introduction Chapter, Sociology _____

2 Number of words in ten lines: __104__

3 Words per line $= \dfrac{\text{Words in ten lines (104)}}{10} =$ __10.4__

4 Number of lines in chapter or article: __250__

5 Number of words = words per line (10.4) × number of lines (250) = __2600__

6 Beginning reading time: __8:00 P.M.__

7 Ending reading time: __8:20 P.M.__

8 Total reading time: __20 minutes__

9 Reading speed per minute $= \dfrac{\text{Total words (2600)}}{\text{Total reading time (20 min)}} =$ __130__

words per minute

4 Become an Active Reader

Unfortunately, many people have the idea that reading is a passive activity, that one reads along and somehow soaks up information from the pages. This attitude is one of the primary reasons why many people have difficulty reading.

Many people say they can't keep up a high level of concentration when they are faced with reading several pages of material. They point out that after a few minutes of reading their minds wander to what happened at home, what they plan to do on vacation, or how nice it will be when they finish their study program. Lack of concentration is a symptom of passive reading.

One way of combating the concentration problem is to become an active reader. It is difficult to lose concentration when you are actively reading because you are doing something, you are participating actively.

No matter what type of material you are reading or for what purpose, it is possible to become an active reader. To become an active reader, ask questions while you read and try to answer them as you go along.

Four Basic Questions[4]

a What is this article, chapter, or book about? In a sentence or two, what is the main theme of the piece of writing you are reading?

b What does the article, chapter, or book say in detail? That is, what are the main ideas and how are they developed?

c Is the content of this article, chapter, or book true? Of course you cannot make up your mind about this until you have answered questions **a** and **b**. And even then you may have difficulty if the piece of reading is in an area that is new to you. Nevertheless you should work at attempting to answer this question.

d Of what value is this article, chapter, or book? This is the "so what" question. What is the significance of the writing? Why does the author think the material is important? Do you think the material is important? Why? Or why not?

Techniques for the Active Reader If you own the book, magazine, or journal you are reading, there are a number of techniques you can use to assist you in your quest to become an active reader.

a Underline or use a show-through marking pen to indicate key words or phrases. Usually it is better to do this after you have read through the material once, so that you can put what you are reading into perspective and can identify the important and the less important. Some persons err by underlining or marking nearly all the material. The key is to be selective, marking only important words or phrases. Words to mark include definitions, items in a list, and main ideas in a paragraph.

b In the margins draw a vertical line adjacent to an important paragraph. Place an asterisk in the margin adjacent to an important sentence; perhaps two asterisks for those sentences that are *key*. If the author is developing several points, number them in the margins. Write key words from the text in the margins. Though gimmicks, these techniques will help you to become an active reader. And further, if you are reading material that you know you will want to review again—for an examination or for some paper you are writing—the clues in the margins can help you greatly in speeding up the review process.

c Write questions or comments in the margins. Carry on a conversation with the author. If you don't understand something you're reading, make a comment to that effect in the margin. If you read something that explains what was hazy on a previous page, note that. If you've read something in another book or journal that is in opposition to what you are now reading, note the other source and the difference of opinion. Think while you read, and note some of your thoughts in the margins.

d When you've finished reading, on the empty pages in the front or the back of the book—if it is a book that you are reading and it is yours—write a paragraph or two of what the book was about. Doing this forces you to reflect back on the content and the meaning of what you've just read. And it also provides you an excellent summary when you wish to come back to this book at some later date, assuming the book becomes part of your personal working library.

Go back and reread this section, "Techniques for the Active Reader," and then mark it following the suggestions given. When you have finished, compare your work with the marked copy below. There is no one correct way to mark reading material, so don't be concerned if your marking is not identical with the example copy.

Techniques for the active reader If you own the book, magazine, or journal you are reading, there are a number of techniques you can use to assist you in your quest to become an active reader.

1.
Mark during second reading

a Underline or use a show-through marking pen to indicate key words or phrases. Usually it is better to do this after you have read through the material once, so that you can put what you are reading into perspective and can identify the important and the less important. Some persons err by underlining or marking nearly all the material. The key is to be selective, marking only important words or phrases.

2.
clues for review

b In the margins draw a vertical line adjacent to an important paragraph. Place an asterisk in the margin adjacent to an important sentence; perhaps two asterisks for those sentences that are *key*. If the author is developing several points, number them in the margins. Write key words from the text in the margins. Though gimmicks, these techniques will help you to become an active reader. And further, if you are reading material that you know you will want to review again—for an examination or for some paper you are writing—the clues in the margins can help you greatly in speeding up the review process.

3.

c Write questions or comments in the margins. Carry on a conversation with the author. If you don't understand something you're reading, make a comment to that effect in the margin. If you read something that explains what was hazy on a previous page, note that. If you've read something in another book or journal that is in opposition to what you are now reading, note the other source and the difference of opinion. Think while you read, and note some of your thoughts in the margins.

4.

d When you've finished reading, on the empty pages in the front or the back of the book—if it is a book that you are reading and it is yours—write a paragraph or two of what the book was about. Doing this forces you to reflect back on the content and the meaning of what you've just read. And it also provides you an excellent summary when you wish to come back to this book at some later date, assuming the book becomes part of your personal working library.

e Take notes while you read. No doubt back in elementary school you learned the rudiments of outlining. If you are comfortable with a formal outlining approach—the type taught in many schools—use it. The formal outline is most easily developed by using the author's order of headings as the major outline entries. The highest-order headings are indicated with roman numerals (I, II, III, etc.), the second-order headings with capital letters (A, B, C, etc.), the third-order headings with arabic numerals (1, 2, 3, etc.), and the fourth-order headings with lowercase letters (a, b, c, etc.).

Rewrite the author's headings into statements that emphasize the main idea of the material that follows the headings. After listing the main ideas, you will often want to include important details such as the definitions of words and supporting data.

If you are less inclined toward a formal outline, you may find it useful to develop a listing of the main ideas and the supporting detail the author is including. For many persons this informal style of note taking is more useful, particularly if you do not want to adhere to the rather rigid requirements imposed by formal outlining.

f Relate what you are reading to your own experiences. One of the advantages you have as a returning student is the many years of experience of living that you bring with you. Use this experience to advantage. Don't, as some students do, feel that you must push your experiences aside as if they hadn't happened.

Reflect on your experiences while you read. Constantly ask if what you are reading is related to something you remember from your work, your family and social life, anywhere at all.

You can often help make reading understandable by using your own experiences as examples of what the author is saying. And often the reading can help you make sense out of experiences you have had but whose meaning you've wondered about. This is particularly so if what you are reading is quite theoretical. One of the purposes of a theory is to help persons make sense out of experience so that some further experiences can be planned with assurance of the outcome. The practical examples of where the theory fits and how it may be applied make the theory come alive.

Again go back to the beginning of the section, "Techniques for the Active Reader." This time take notes on the section, and record them in the space below. When you have finished, compare your notes with the example. But again realize there are many "correct" ways of taking notes when reading. Use whatever style is comfortable for you, and gets you involved in the reading.

Notes from Reading

EXAMPLE NOTES

Techniques for the active reader
   1 Underline key words and phrases
       Underline during second reading
       Be selective
   2 Mark what is important
       Vertical lines by important paragraphs
       Asterisks by important sentences
       Numbers by sequence of points
   3 Write questions or comments in margins
       Conversation with author
       Note thoughts about material
   4 When finished reading, write statement of what book is about

---

5 Learn about the Author of the Material You Are Reading

If you can learn something about the author's age, his or her education, the kinds of jobs held, and the kind of writing he or she has done, you can draw some conclusions about the author's perspective and biases.

For example, if you know the author is a student of Marxist writing and has written other material on that general theme, you have some idea of what to expect in the material you are about to read.

If when you are reading about how humans learn, you discover that the author has been a student of B. F. Skinner and subscribes to Skinner's theories, you know something about what to expect.

If you discover that the author was born and raised in England and lives there now, you will expect a somewhat different perspective than if the person lived in this country.

Knowing something about the person's background, experience, and education can give you some perspective. However, it is also important to read with as open a mind as possible about the author. The author may have changed considerably since publishing a book 10 years earlier.

Realize, though, that articles and textbooks, poems and plays, and everything else that is written are written by human beings. As absurd as it sounds, some readers appear to lose sight of this fact. Everyone has emotions and goals and needs to earn a living. Knowing something about the author whose work we are reading gives us a perspective on the person as a human being.

6 Improve Your Vocabulary

If you are reading in an area of study new to you, there is a good chance that many words will be new to you. Until the new words are learned, reading will be difficult. Chapter 6 outlines several steps you can follow to improve your vocabulary.

7 Read Broadly

One time, as a part of a class discussion I was leading, I asked each student, in turn, to share the names of the books or magazine articles he or she had recently read and to tell a little bit about what he or she had gotten out of the material. I had anticipated hearing references to recently acclaimed novels, to articles in the *New Yorker* or the *Saturday Review,* and so on.

All the students in the class were advanced graduate students working on Ph.D. degrees in continuing education. With but a few exceptions the answers surprised me. The vast majority of these students were reading nothing beyond the readings suggested for their courses and what they needed for the research they were doing in their graduate programs. They were not reading novels. They were not reading thoughtful nonfiction writing outside their field of specialization. They read no poetry.

During the discussion we talked about why this was so, why the students weren't reading more broadly. The answer that several gave was lack of time. Most of them were returning students who had family and work responsibility beyond their graduate study responsibility. They did have limited time for other reading.

But a second reason several students mentioned bothered me. These students said they could see no good reason for reading a novel. They were social scientists, and reading fiction—something that was obviously not true—was something a social scientist shouldn't do. They also said: ''This is an age of specialists. Why should we bother reading outside our area of specialization?''

In fairness to the class, not all the students held this attitude. Several argued the importance of reading broadly, both in fiction and in nonfiction outside the students' immediate area of professional specialization. These students pointed out how novelists, for example, through their creative use of the written language deal with questions before scientists do. They also mentioned how novelists are able to deal with whole pictures, showing the relationship of parts to the whole, while scientists must deal with more isolated concepts that can be more closely controlled.

Finally, this minority of students argued that a broadened reading program, to encompass all forms of writing—fiction, poetry, plays, and nonfiction outside of the area of specialization—will assist the student who wishes to put what he or she is reading into a broader perspective. Not only does reading broadly give a wider perspective, these students argued, but it also allows a person to see where a specialization fits in. This minority of students didn't argue against specialization; they argued for specialization with perspective. A broadened reading program would provide this perspective.

One interesting starting place, if you wish to systematically broaden your reading, is to read Clifton Fadiman's *The Lifetime Reading Plan.*[5] Just as you set aside time each day for study and reading of materials related to your course work, set aside time for recreational reading, perhaps before you go to sleep at night, first thing in the morning, or when you've finished lunch. It doesn't matter when. But if you can work out a specific time within your daily schedule, the reading will get done. Waiting to do recreational reading during vacation time, though a good idea, is not the answer. Reading for a half hour a day, every day, will result in completing many times more reading.

HOW TO READ FOR DIFFERENT PURPOSES

Earlier in this chapter we said that knowing the purpose for reading determines how fast you will read and in large part sets the stage for becoming an active reader.

We will look at four purposes for reading and give some directions on how you can most effectively do each. We will not discuss recreational reading. In no way is this omission to imply that recreational reading is not important. It is of great importance, as we have argued above. And many of the suggestions that are related below, in reference to the other reading purposes, will also be of assistance to you when you do recreational reading.

Because the majority of the reading you will do is nonfictional—articles, books, chapters in books, research reports—the focus of this section will be on reading this type of writing.

READING FOR INFORMATION

There are four situations in which we read for information, depending on the type of information we are seeking. (We are considering only nonfictional material).

1 Reading for the Overview of a Book

A mistake many students make, particularly if they are assigned entire books to read or are offered a reading list with several alternative books, is to select a book and then begin reading it on the first page. A much more efficient way of reading is to first get an overview of the book. How does one go about doing this?

Turn to the title page. Note the complete title. Often a book will have a subtitle that will tell you more about the book's content than does the title. You will also learn the author's name and the publisher of the book from the title page.

Check the copyright. The copyright date is usually printed on the page immediately following the title page. This page, in recent years, also often includes Library of Congress Cataloging Data. In brief form, this information categorizes the book into a topic area. For example, the book *The Practice of Continuing Education in the Human Services,* by Armand Lauffer,[6] has this Library of Congress Cataloging Data printed on the copyright page:

Includes Index.
1. Mental Hygiene—Study and Teaching (Continuing Education).

The Courage to Create by Rollo May[7] includes this Library of Congress information on the copyright page:

Includes Bibliographical References.
1. Creation (Literary, Artistic, etc.).

Read the author's preface or introduction. This will tell you something of why the author wrote the book, often how the book is organized, and what some of the important topics are that the author hopes to cover.

Browse through the table of contents. This will give you the structure for the book in some detail by listing the main topics covered by chapters.

Page through the index. Note the range of terms that is used in the book and terms that are unfamiliar to you.

Check the bibliography if the book has one. Here you can see the range of references that the book uses. You may recognize many of them if you have read previously in this field.

Read the publisher's statement on the dust cover (if the book has one). Though this statement is obviously written to capture the attention of someone browsing through a bookstore, it is often a good summary of the book's contents.

Read the "about the author" statement. This usually appears on the dust cover, but is sometimes included in one of the last pages of a book. Here you can learn about the background of the author and the experiences he or she had that relate to the topic of the book.

Select one or two chapters that seem central to the main topic the book covers. Read the first paragraph or two of the chapters, and read the summary paragraph at the end of the chapters. Note the headings scattered through the chapters to see how the topic is organized.

All of this can be done in less than a half hour and sometimes in 15 minutes when you get good at it.

You may discover, once you've taken the overview, that the book isn't worth reading any further, the topic isn't what you thought it was, or you need read only one or two of its chapters to obtain the information you want. Until you've done the overview reading, you can't answer these questions.

You may discover that you do indeed want to spend considerable time with the book. Not only has the overview reading provided you with this information, but it also has given you some broad information that will help you put your reading of the book into perspective.

Select one of the books you are required to read and complete the following:

Name of Book (Include subtitle, if any): _____

_____

Author(s): _____

Copyright Date (Choose most recent date if several are listed): _____

Preface: Are author's reasons for writing the book given? _____
What are the reasons? _____
_____

Does preface explain organization of book? _____ How is book organized? _____
_____

Table of Contents: How many chapters in the book? _____
Outline major sections _____
_____
_____
_____

Index: Look for unfamiliar terms _____
_____

Bibliography: Does book have one? _____
Appendixes: If present, what are topics? _____
_____

Publisher's Statement on Dust Cover: If present, what does publisher say about book's contents? _____
_____
_____

"About the Author" Statement: Experience of author related to topic of book? _____
_____

Review One or Two Chapters: Do chapters have summary statements? _____ Are there study questions at end of chapters? _____
Do chapters include pictures? Maps? Graphs? Or other illustrative material? _____ Are subheadings used for emphasis? _____ Do introductory paragraphs tell what chapters are about? _____

2 Reading for the Overview of a Chapter or an Article

The same principles outlined above may be applied to the reading of shorter writings. When reading a chapter of a book or an article in a magazine or journal, first read it in overview.

Determine the relationship of the chapter or the article to other chapters or articles in the document you are reading. What kind of journal or magazine is it? What kind of book is it in which the chapter appears?

Determine the structure of the article or chapter. Read the headings, the signposts the author uses to show the reader the organization of the piece. Determine the relationship of the ideas in the writing by noting the levels of headlines. Which are the main ideas, and which are the subideas?

Look for introductory and summary paragraphs. In a few sentences, these key paragraphs will tell you what is the main topic of the article or chapter.

3   Reading to Find Specific Answers

The word *scanning* is often used to describe this process. Say you are searching for the date that Lincoln gave his Gettysburg Address. Rather than go to an encyclopedia and read every word in an article about the Gettysburg Address, scan through the article for dates. In a couple of minutes you should be able to find the answer to your question.

This process of scanning is not a new technique to any of you. When you are checking the spelling of a word in the dictionary, you quickly scan through until you find the word. When you are looking for a telephone number, you scan until you find the name you want.

But for some reason, when it comes to reading so-called academic material, many students believe they must read every word. It's not necessary. Know what you are searching for, and look for it as rapidly as you can, not worrying about all the "good information" you are passing over on the way to finding the answer to your question.

One practical technique to follow when scanning is to fix the question in your mind, then run your eyes as fast as you can down the columns of print until you find the answer. The key is keeping the question fixed in your mind. Don't be enticed away from your question when your eyes spot a topic that looks interesting. If the reading columns are narrow, say, of newspaper width, practice running your eyes down the center of the column.

Make use of headings, indentations, and italicized words in searching for your answers. These will often give you clues about where the information you are seeking is located. And always keep focused in your mind the question or fact you are searching for. If you find yourself falling into the trap of reading every word, stop and start over again, giving yourself a new "fix" on the question you want answered.

4   Reading for Directions

An obvious kind of information you may wish to get from reading is how to do something. How to write a research proposal, how to do a laboratory experiment, and so on. We suggested above you should scan down the page of material as quickly as possible to answer a question. When reading directions on how to do something you must usually read every word. Every words must be read several times if the directions are rather poorly written.

Reading for information is a major part of any student's work, yet too often students read all material in the same way. By learning how to read for overview, by learning how to read for facts, and by learning how to concentrate when reading directions, you can greatly improve your overall reading program. Also, reading for overview is usually the first step to accomplish before doing more intensive reading on a topic.

READING FOR UNDERSTANDING

A variety of terms are used to describe reading for understanding: *thorough reading, reading completely, mastering the material. Studying* is the most common term used, although studying can and should involve more than reading.

How can I get more out of what I read? is a question many people ask. For students this often is translated to mean, "How can I glean enough from my reading to pass the examinations?"

Some persons attempt to answer the question, How can I get more out of what I read? by trying to memorize what they are reading. But without a systematic way of reading, without some planning, and without active involvement with the reading material, it is difficult to know if you are memorizing the important material. The question then becomes, How can I recognize what is important so I can proceed to memorize that material?

First, let's set aside memorization for the time being at least. There is a considerable difference between memorizing and understanding. We can memorize without understanding. We can memorize long lists of definitions and pages of formulas without understanding them. Here we are talking about reading for understanding; reading so you "know" what you are reading; and reading so that the material read is part of you, you can reformulate it in your own words, and you are comfortable that you aren't distorting the author's meaning.

If you are able to read for understanding, then you don't have to worry about memorizing. Memorization as a technique becomes irrelevant. When you understand the material you are reading, you are well past the stage of memorization. You know the material far better than had you only memorized it.

How do you read for understanding? What procedures should you follow?

How to Read for Understanding

The procedure suggested here, a series of questions, applies to all nonfiction writing whether it be an article in a journal, a chapter in a book, or an entire book.

1 What, in overview, is the writing about? Before beginning to read for understanding, first read for the overview. Refer to the previous section for the process of overview reading.

2 What question or questions is the author attempting to answer? Complete this step of the process by turning each heading into a question. By paying attention to the levels of the headings, you can determine the major and the secondary questions the author is asking.

3 What important terms does the author use? These terms may appear in the headings. Sometimes they appear in boldface type; sometimes they are italicized; sometimes they appear in the opening sentences of paragraphs.

4 How does the author define these key terms? For example, you may be reading an article criticizing education in this country. *Education* is obviously a key word the author will be using. But how does the author define the word? There is no general agreement. Some people use the word to describe something a person attains. Others define the word as the process by which one learns something. Still others define the word both of these ways—as an attainment and as a process for attaining. To understand what the author is talking about, to understand the questions that are raised, the reader must know how the author is defining the word.

The author may write, "I define education to be . . ." But often the reader must define the word out of the context of the material—how the word is used—and without examples describing the word.

5 What answers does the author give to the questions raised? Here is where understanding the structure of nonfiction writing can be helpful. Paragraphs are the building blocks. And within a paragraph there are usually three kinds of statements: (a) a topic sentence, which is the main idea for the paragraph; (b) supporting material, statements that restate the topic sentence, illustrate it, or amplify it some way, and (c) a summary sentence that says again what was said in the paragraph. Not all paragraphs are written in exactly this fashion. Sometimes the topic sentence is also the summary sentence and appears at the end of the paragraph. Sometimes there is no one topic sentence, but phrases in several sentences contribute to the topic or main idea of the paragraph. Sometimes the topic is sufficiently broad that several paragraphs are written about it, with subtopics within each paragraph.

By knowing this inner structure of writing, you have some clues to how a writer goes about answering the questions that are raised. Also, by knowing the structure followed by most good writers, you are able to sort out what is central and important from that which is more detailed, illustrative, and supportive.

6 What questions does the author raise but perhaps answer incompletely or maybe not at all?

7 What is the author's point of view? All writers have a point of view, even if they claim to be completely objective and without bias. Sometimes writers will openly state the assumptions that guide their work. If they do, you then know their point of view. Of course you must be alert in your reading to see if what they are writing is consistent with the assumptions they have stated. Also, reading the preface or introduction of a book— which you should have done during the overview stage of reading—can give you some valuable information about the writer's point of view. This is also true of the information that may be included concerning the author.

Another way of detecting the author's point of view is to read material on the same topic by another author. Often instructors will assign readings that appear to duplicate one another. What they are usually doing is providing you with an opportunity to read several points of view on the same topic, recognizing that authors do have biases when they write.

8 How does what the author says relate to your experience and other reading? From what you know of the topic you are reading—what you have learned from other reading in the general area and, as important, what you have experienced in your life—how does what the author is saying compare? Does what the author has written make sense according to your experience? One way to check is to attempt to give specific examples of what the author is saying from your own experience. Of course you cannot always do this. You may be reading in a new area where you have had no experience and where you have done no other reading, so thinking back to examples in your life experience is impossible. But this is the exception. Almost everything you read, if you think about it for a moment, has some relationship to something you have experienced in your life. This is of course one of the advantages mature adults bring to anything they do. With experience, even though somewhat remote from the reading you are doing, you can often bring the reading into focus. You can better understand something new if you can relate it to something specific you have experienced.

Of course, this is also one of the basic differences between memorizing and understanding. One can memorize without ever trying to relate the material to what one has experienced. But to understand material, to make it part of you, part of your experience, relating the new material to previous experience is an important step.

Attempting to relate your reading to previous reading and experience is also an active process, another approach to moving you from being a passive, nonparticipating reader to an actively involved reader who questions the material. It is another way of carrying on a conversation with the author of the material. What you are doing, in effect, is saying to the author, "Say, I did something like that a few years ago, and what you are writing here is related." Or you might say: "I read an article or a book about that topic last year. You're using different words, but you're talking about the same thing."

READING CRITICALLY

What does it mean to read critically? When does someone read with this purpose in mind?

First, to read critically doesn't mean you are trying only to find fault with what you are reading. When you read critically, you are also interested in discovering the good points.

When you read critically, you make a judgment about what you are reading. You may take three positions concerning the material you are reading:

1 You agree with it.
2 You disagree with it.
3 You suspend judgment about it.[8]

Of course there may be some combination of these positions. That is, you may agree with some of it, disagree with some of it, and suspend judgment—not take a position—on some of it.

Before Reading Critically

Before you can read something critically, you must understand it. It must make sense to you. You must know what the author is talking about. Thus a requisite for reading critically is reading for understanding, to come to grips with the author so that you can say, "Yes, I know what he or she is talking about."

Of course there is much critical comment made of writing before the reader really understands what the author has said. Too often, in our society, people are prone to criticize based on what someone else has said about the writing. They haven't read it themselves, and yet they feel they can make a critical comment about the material. It is as if you criticized your neighbor's wallpaper based on a friend's judgment about it, and you never saw it yourself.

Many people today make judgments about books based on a review they have read. It seems absurd that anyone could believe he or she could make a critical comment about a piece of writing without even reading it.

Another type of critical comment is often made by a person who reads some material and then says, "I disagree with this material." When asked why, the person responds, "Because I don't understand it."

After you have carefully read the material and have made every attempt at understanding it, you may then comment on the difficulty of understanding it. But this is hardly a reason for disagreeing with it. More appropriately you might say that you have to withhold judgment because you weren't able to understand the material.

Another belief many people hold is that all disagreement is based on a lack of understanding. If you can get two people to understand something, then they will no longer be in disagreement.

Sometimes this is the case. People do seem to disagree because they don't understand something in the same way. It would be better, though, if we referred to this problem more accurately and called it a *misunderstanding* or a *lack of understanding* rather than a *disagreement*.

For a true disagreement to occur, both parties must first understand each other. They must know as fully as possible what each other is saying. Or, in our case here, the reader must know as fully as possible what the author has written. Until this level of understanding is achieved, it is not possible for an honest disagreement to take place.

To speak to the other side of the question for a moment, it is also impossible to agree with an author until you as fully as possible understand what he or she has written. It is unfounded agreement if when asked why you agree with a writer, you answer, "It sounds right to me." That's not enough of a reason. Why does it sound right? What specifically about what has been written do you agree with and why?

Feelings are an important part of the response. That is, you may say that you feel good about reading the material. But beyond the feeling level, what specifically about the writing caused you to agree with it?

Often the material you read will be new or relatively new to you. This may present a problem if you want to read critically. You must, through careful reading and deliberation, bring yourself up to the level of the author. Of course this is impossible in many ways. The author may have spent a lifetime researching the material he or she is writing about, and to expect you to come up to that level in a few hours or even in a few days is absurd.

But it is possible to move toward the goal of being where the author is, particularly with the piece of writing you are reading, if you work at trying to understand the material. After all, although the person may have spent a lifetime researching the topic, the author is not sitting on a throne with the readers all kneeling around it. The author is another human being trying to communicate some ideas to you with the hope that you will understand them. And until you understand the ideas, you have no right to be critical of them.

When Do You Read Critically?

A quick answer is that you should read critically all the time. But this is impractical. Sometimes you may be looking for the answer to a specific question. To read critically and comment on the material makes no sense.

In the press of time, you may not have the opportunity to read critically all the assignments that face you. As we said earlier, some of these assignments you will read quickly, sometimes even scanning through them to get the main ideas. Others you will read more carefully, attempting to understand the material as thoroughly as possible. And some selected readings you will want to read critically. But which ones?

I would suggest that the readings most important to the course you are taking, to the writing assignment you are working on, to the research project you may be working on are the ones you may wish to read critically.

The process of reading critically is an extremely active process. To do an adequate job of reading material critically, you may be forced to read the material several times. And through the process of attempting to make a judgment about the material, you will find that your understanding of the material deepens. Though a few paragraphs ago I said that understanding was a prerequisite to doing critical reading, critical reading itself directly contributes to deeper understanding.

If you are given the assignment of writing a book review or commenting critically on a research report, you are faced with having to read critically. Too often people face the task of writing a book review by writing a book *report*. They write about what is in the book, but they don't make judgments about the writing. In fact one can write a book report without even getting to the ''reading for understanding'' stage. The same goes for writing comments about a research report: the student may merely report what the research was about without making any judgments about the work.

A Process for Critical Reading

How do you do critical reading? What are some principles to be followed?

1 Separate knowledge from opinion. As you read the material, constantly look for supporting evidence. Ask such questions as: ''Why is this so?'' ''How can the author say this?'' ''What support does the author have for these comments?'' The difference between knowledge and opinion is that knowledge is supported while opinion is not.

What are various kinds of support? The author may support a position through logical argument. Or the author may have actually observed a situation and is sharing the results of that observation. The author may be relying on others who have researched and written in the field to support the arguments made. The author may share an insight gained through a series of events and activities he or she has experienced.

2 Determine the author's assumptions. On what givens is the writing based? Often in the preface or introduction and sometimes in the comments about the author will be information about what the author assumes.

For example, if the author is writing about an economic problem, he or she may assume that economic growth is foundational to any economic system. Another writer on the same topic may assume a no-growth status for a future economic system. The two pieces of writing will obviously be quite different from each other. And the basic reason they are different is that they start with very different assumptions.

Often as a critical reader, you need to derive the assumptions from the material you are reading. The author may not be explicit in stating them.

Unless you determine the author's assumptions at the very outset, you may find yourself disliking the material and not realizing that this is because you disagree with the assumptions. Doing this is certainly acceptable if you are reading recreationally. But you cannot read material critically if the basis for a disagreement you have is the author's assumptions. Assumptions are givens. You must find out what they are, and then, for the purpose of critical reading, you must accept them.

3 Determine the author's perspective. What are the author's biases? What have been the author's experiences? What kind of formal training has the author had? How old is the author? Where did the author grow up and go to school? Answers to these questions will give you some clues to the perspective the author may hold. Even though some authors claim to be objective in their writing, this position is impossible. All of us have biases. Even when we believe we are totally objective, we are not and cannot be. What an author writes is influenced by his or her background of experience; it cannot be otherwise.

4 Determine if you are in agreement, are in disagreement, or must withhold judgment about the writing. If you decide that you disagree with part or much of the writing, carefully consider your reasons for disagreement. Four basic reasons for disagreement are that (a) the writer is uninformed, (b) the writer is misinformed, (c) the writer is not logical with argumentation, or (d) the analysis is incomplete.

If you believe the writer is uninformed, then you must be able to show specifically what information is missing and why the missing information is important to the position the author is taking. Perhaps you have recently read a piece of research that relates directly to what the author is saying, but the author hasn't mentioned it. If you believe this piece of research puts an entirely different slant on what the author is saying, then you are in a position to say that that author is, at least in this area, uninformed. But you must be specific. You must have specific information that you can cite which will support your point.

To say that a writer is misinformed is a more difficult task. If you believe the author is misinformed, you are obligated to show where the author's information is inaccurate. For example, the author may be using a research report to support a position taken. Let's assume that the research report is grossly inaccurate. Probably unknowingly, the author is thus misinformed and is using inaccurate information to make a point. A legitimate position for you as a critic is to point out the specifics of the information, with sufficient evidence to show why the research report the author used is not accurate.

Showing that the author is illogical with argumentation takes careful work. Basically there are two ways in which an author may be illogical: (1) drawing conclusions that do not follow from the statements offered and (2) being inconsistent or contradictory in stating positions.

Let's look at the first, drawing conclusions that do not follow from the statements offered. Such conclusions are often referred to as *non sequiturs.* Let's say the author makes the following points: (1) The supply of natural gas in the United States is decreasing. (2) The supply of coal would seem to be sufficient to last for at least 200 years, maybe more. (3) The oil supply, like that of natural gas, is also limited.

The author of these statements, then concludes, "Given this information about our supplies of coal, natural gas, and oil, we should each try to grow more of our own food." The conclusion cannot be drawn from the premises presented.

As a critic searching for non sequiturs in arguments, you search for argumentation that follows the above illogical development. If you find such examples, you are required to show how the conclusions reached do not derive from the statements offered.

Contradictions are sometimes easily spotted in writing, but often they are hidden and take considerable digging to ferret out. For example, on page 23 an author may say, "Most people, in order to succeed, need considerable outside imposed motivators such as salary incentives." Later, on page 53, the author writes: "One assumption we can make about human nature is the inward drive that people have. This inward drive is stronger than any outside influence persons face."

On reflection you as the critical reader must ask: "Which is it? Are people mostly directed by inward forces or mostly influenced by so-called imposed motivators? As a careful critic you will point out this contradiction in your analysis of the writing.

If after careful reading, you discover that you cannot show where the author is uninformed, where misinformed, or where illogical, then you have no basis for disagreement with the author. But you may wish to make a statement about what the author has not done. You may wish to argue that the author has incompletely covered the topic or has incompletely analyzed the problem. But you must be able to do so by showing specifically how the author has not used some of the evidence at hand to make a point. You must be able to show *how* a more complete analysis of the material might have taken the author further.

Of course every piece of writing might be taken further. You as a critical reader are placed in the position of using your judgment to show how the writing would have been more complete, and likely more important, if the author had done certain specific things to carry the analysis further. It is not a legitimate criticism simply to say that the writing is incomplete, for in a sense all writing is to some extent incomplete.

READING TO CREATE

You will often be faced with a term paper assignment that requires reading many sources: books, chapters from books, journals, popular magazines, and so on. This task can be pure drudgery, or it can be one of the most creative things you have ever done. In the chapter on writing we will discuss approaches to writing term papers and similar kinds of reports. Here we will discuss how you might go about reading with the purpose of creating something new, with the purpose of finding an answer to a question that may not have been answered before.

I am beginning with the assumptions that (1) it is possible to create new knowledge from knowledge that already exists, from writings that are already available to you, and (2) there is a specific process of reading to create something new. Reading to create assumes that you already know how to read to obtain an overview of materials, that you have the ability to read for understanding, and that you are able to read critically. The skills of doing these types of reading will be extremely helpful as you proceed to this highest level of reading, reading to create.

A Process for Reading to Create

1 As carefully as possible define the problem or the question you want to answer. A basic difference between reading to create and the other types of reading we have discussed is the focus. Where previously we showed how to focus on the author and what questions he or she raised, now the focus changes. Rather than being on the author, the focus is on you, the reader. What specifically do you want answered? What question do you have? Go as far as you can in specifically stating the question you want answered. But do not be disappointed if you find you cannot define

the question as carefully as you would like. One important dimension of the process of creative reading is its dynamic nature. You will likely find that the question you originally framed can be sharpened as you read. In fact, once you begin reading to find answers to your original question, you may find that you want to substantially change the question you want answered. On the one hand, this can be frustrating. But on the other hand, this is an exciting dimension of creative reading. To deal with the frustration of changing your question after you begin reading requires a certain amount of openness and flexibility on your part.

2 Develop a bibliography. List all the writings you can find by searching the library for resource materials. (See Chapter 7, "Using Resources Effectively.") Your bibliography will include books, magazines, journals, and so on.

3 Do an overview reading of the materials on the list. There are several obvious reasons for this. The list will likely be much longer than you can possibly work through in a reasonable time if you assume that you are going to read everything completely. And further, many of the items on the list may not fit your topic as closely as their titles suggest. So do an overview reading of the materials, weeding out those that do not apply to your question. Also, at this stage of the process you may find that you can rewrite your original question more specifically.

Begin to select passages that are most relevant to the question you are trying to answer. When you are first sorting through the maze of materials on your bibliography, you may find it difficult to select the most relevant passages. But after you have looked at several books and have glanced through several journal articles, you should be able to identify those passages that hold the most promise. It is a bit dangerous to identify the most important passages at the very beginning of your overview reading because you may change your original question; you surely will refine it after some initial searching. Thus at the beginning you can't know which passages to identify for careful reading.

4 Be clear about the meaning of terms. Let's say you are writing a paper on how to provide educational programs for the elderly. Some of the terms you will likely be using and need to be clear about are *educational programs, elderly* (what ages are included), and *learning,* to mention but three. It's important to do this because various authors may be talking about the same thing but using different terms. What you want is a common base, and your definitions will provide this basis for searching. You want to have a common set of meanings to which you can apply all the material you are reading. And you must read carefully to determine if what a particular author is talking about, even though different terms are used, fits the terms you are using.

Another danger to look out for is the author who uses terms that are identical to yours, but means something different. If you are studying in the social sciences or education you will see this problem often occurring. For example, a given author may refer to learning as a change in behavior, another may talk about learning as the accumulation of information, and still a third may define learning as personal growth. All three of these authors use the word *learning* in their writings, yet without knowing how they define the word you will be misled. Each author is using the same word to describe quite different situations.

5 Write a set of subquestions. As you do the overall reading of the materials in the bibliography, you should be able to refine your original question or topic to the point of writing several subquestions about it. These subquestions will direct your reading once they are developed. They will provide you with a framework for going to the passages you have identified.

6 Search for the answers. Now you are ready to begin a systematic reading of the passages you have identified, to search for the answers to the questions you have raised. Of course as you do this you must keep in mind the problem of terms discussed earlier. You must also be aware of context, that is, do not pull out an answer without considering what came before and what came after it.

Often you will find contradicting answers to your questions. At first this can be frustrating. What do you do: reject those answers that seem to be a minority position on a question or include all the answers? A guide to follow is to include all the answers, whether they are in agreement with each other or not. But when you do this, make certain, insofar as you can, that the author is defining the terms the same way you do. What at first glance may appear to be a difference of opinion may be resolved when you discover that the writer is defining terms differently from the way you are.

7 Analyze answers and draw conclusions. This is probably the most creative part of the entire process and the part that many readers do poorly or not at all. You are stopping short of creative reading if you find several answers to a question you have raised and only note them.

The creative activity begins when you set down the different answers, those that are in agreement with each other and those that differ, and then carefully and systematically compare the answers. Stopping at this point in the process can be very useful, as several sources of answers are brought together to answer a question. But the process can be taken further. What can you conclude from the reading you've done? What answer or answers to the questions you have raised can you support, allowing that there may be differences of opinion reflected in the readings? Can you draw a conclusion from the various answers you've discovered? When you get this far with the process you are becoming a truly creative reader, for you are creating new knowledge (answers) that is greater than any one of the answers you have read. You are creating something new that transcends the reading you have done.

The process may even take you to the point where you are able to derive answers to your questions that are not directly related to any of the answers you found in the readings, but are more complete and elegant. In effect the readings you have done have combined with your own personal experience, and through a process of creative thinking you have come up with creative answers.[9]

Creative reading is the most advanced process of reading, likely the most difficult, but at the same time the most exciting. You are not only required to have mastered the ability to read to get information, to understand, and to be critical, but you must also relate readings from several sources to questions that you raise.

SUMMARY

In this chapter we have discussed seven principles for improving your reading: (1) read with a purpose, (2) determine type and quality of material, (3) adjust reading speed to purpose and type of material, (4) become an active reader, (5) learn about the author of the material, (6) improve your vocabulary, and (7) read broadly.

Specific suggestions are offered for reading with four broad purposes in mind: (1) reading for information, (2) reading for understanding, (3) reading critically, and (4) reading to create. Each of these purposes builds on the others. For example, to do creative reading you must be able to do the other three types of reading.

REFERENCES

1 Mortimer J. Adler and Charles Van Doren, *How to Read a Book,* Simon & Schuster, New York, 1972.

2 Francis Bacon, *Essays and New Atlantis,* Walter J. Black, Roslyn, N.Y., 1942, pp. 207–208.

3 Alton L. Raygor and George B. Schick, *Reading at Efficient Rates,* McGraw-Hill, New York, 1970, pp. 68–69.

4 Adapted from Adler and Van Doren, op. cit., pp. 46–47.

5 Clifton Fadiman, *The Lifetime Reading Plan,* World, Cleveland, 1960.

6 Armand Lauffer, *The Practice of Continuing Education in the Human Services,* McGraw-Hill, New York, 1977.

7 Rollo May, *The Courage to Create,* Norton, New York, 1975.

8 Adler and Van Doren, op. cit., pp. 137–167.

9 See Chapter 5, "Improve Your Thinking Ability," particularly the section that discusses creative thinking, for a description of the process by which new ideas are created.

CHAPTER 4

BECOME A
BETTER WRITER

We can't avoid writing. It is as much a part of our lives as eating and breathing. We write letters to our friends, instructions to our children, messages to the mechanic who repairs our car, and notes to our children's teachers. Some of us write letters to the editor. We write reports of meetings we attend. Many of us write memos and sales reports. Scarcely a day passes that we don't write something.

Writing will also demand much of your time as a student, second only to reading. You will likely be asked to write one or more of the following:

1 *Report* A description of an experiment or some activity that you observed or in which you participated.

2 *Theme* A short paper usually part of an English course and designed to help improve your writing skills.

3 *Essay* A paper in which you argue a point of view, say, one side of a contemporary issue.

4 *Critical Review* A paper in which you carefully analyze and criticize a book, an article, a research report, a film, a speech, a TV program, or some other form of communication.

5 *Research Report* An account of research activity you conducted. It usually includes a description of the research problem, the research approach used, the findings, and the conclusions and implications of the research.

6 *Term Paper* A documented piece of writing that explores a topic in depth.

7 *Thesis or dissertation*   Usually a requirement for graduate students. It often takes the form of a comprehensive research report, but is longer and more complex than the research report described above.

You may also be asked to write poetry, plays, short stories, and other projects as a requirement of certain courses. And finally, you will likely be asked to write examinations.

In this chapter we will concentrate on improving your writing generally. The focus will be on how to improve writing of papers such as themes, essays, reports, and term papers. We will not discuss writing of theses or dissertations; this will be mentioned in Chapter 8. Nor will we discuss how to write poetry, plays, short stories, or novels. This is not to say that these writing forms are not important, for indeed they are. But this type of writing requires extended discussion and goes beyond the purposes of this book. Not all of you will write poems or short stories, but all of you will write papers of one kind or another.

What can you do to improve your writing? What can you do to make your task of student writing both easier and more interesting?

WRITING PROBLEMS

Let's begin by looking at some of the problems returning students have with writing.

Attitude

Many students, for a variety of reasons, have a negative attitude toward writing. Some believe that our society is becoming dependent on nonwritten forms of communication, such as TV, radio, movies, tape recorders, and the like, and that in a few years the written word will be essentially obsolete. Why be concerned about writing?

Others have a negative attitude because they lack the basic skills of writing. They may have had inadequate writing preparation in their primary and secondary schools, and today writing is difficult for them.

Still others fear being evaluated. They don't want their instructors and their peers to know they have difficulty using written words to communicate. They may also fear having someone read their ideas and then disagree with them.

Writing to Impress

Many students (professors and others too) believe they must write to impress others. As a result their writing often succeeds in confusing rather than communicating. This type of writing takes several forms.

1 Polysyllabic words and go-together words are used. You must read these often new and strange words in context, for they usually have a meaning that is more than the sum of the parts. Examples of these words, sometimes borrowed from government but often invented on college campuses, include *multinational, holistic planning, meaningful relationship, impact study, behavioral objectives,* and *capture the data.* Incidentally, what does one use to capture data—a net, some type of trap, or a posse of researchers?

2 New jargon words and combinations of words are often used. At first glance these words and word combinations sound impressive, but upon reflection we wonder about their meaning, if any. For example, it's possible to construct some high-sounding word combinations from the word lists below. Simply combine a word in column 1 with a word in column 2 and a word in column 3. To make it easy, think of any three-digit number, say, 348. We come up with *systematized reciprocal hardware.* Impressive? Yes. But what does it mean?

3 Sentences are long and often contain several ideas. Many persons, not only students and others associated with universities, are plagued with this writing problem. One of the reasons this problem is so serious is that many persons who write this way believe this is *good* writing. These persons erroneously believe they are displaying their superior knowledge and intelligence by writing long, complicated sentences that contain several ideas.

Edwin Newman discussed this problem in his delightful book *Strictly Speaking.* Newman quotes from a December 1966 working paper developed by Hampshire College in South Amherst, Massachusetts, that says in part:

BUILDING IMPRESSIVE PHRASES*

Column 1	Column 2	Column 3
1 Integrated	**1** Management	**1** Options
2 Total	**2** Organizational	**2** Flexibility
3 Systematized	**3** Monitored	**3** Capability
4 Parallel	**4** Reciprocal	**4** Mobility
5 Functional	**5** Logistical	**5** Programming
6 Responsive	**6** Transitional	**6** Concept
7 Optional	**7** Digital	**7** Projection
8 Synchronized	**8** Incremental	**8** Hardwarde
9 Compatible	**9** Policy	**9** Contingency

* Jerry Apps, *Tips for Article Writers,* Wisconsin Regional Writer's Association, Madison, Wisconsin, 1973, pp. 50–51.

---

that social structure should optimally be the consonant patterned expression of culture; that higher education is enmeshed in a congeries of social and political change; that the field of the humanities suffers from a surfeit of leeching, its blood drawn out by verbalism, explication of text, Alexandrian scholasticism, and the exquisite preciosities and pretentiousness of contemporary literary criticism. [1]

In a research proposal, a professor of economics wrote the following in justifying the need for his project: "Analysis of the conceptual relationships among equity, autonomy, cost and incidence—and empirical work on the magnitudes involved for specific types of programs—would be useful in designing and choosing an appropriate system of school finance."

That paragraph requires some study to extract the meaning.

The following example is taken from a research report: "There appears to be no general consensus in the literature to support the premise that adult learning takes place in formal settings at about the same frequency in rural and urban areas—at least within the context of formal credit programs; however, there appears to be no general consensus that it does not." The researcher wrote fifty-three words to say that he or she didn't find out anything about the research problem that was raised.

This is not a new problem. John Dewey, no doubt one of the most important educational philosophers of all time, wrote the following about the significance of geography and history:

> Surely no better way could be devised of instilling a genuine sense of the part which mind has to play in life than a study of history which makes plain how the entire advance of humanity from savagery to civilization has been dependent upon intellectual discoveries and inventions, and the extent to which the things which ordinarily figure most largely in historical writings have been side issues, or even obstructions for intelligence to overcome. [2]

Dewey offers a powerful idea in that terribly long and involved sentence. But one has to read it more than once to grasp what is being said.

Many additional problems could be listed, but the ones listed above seem to occur often and are particularly troublesome for returning students.

Given that you want to improve your writing, what, then, are some specific suggestions?

IMPROVING READABILITY

As a writer you have two primary concerns, having something to say and being able to say it. Many persons have much to say, but they have difficulty saying it. Occasionally, but not often, a person has the ability to communicate but doesn't have anything to say. And of course it is not too unusual to find people who neither have anything to say nor know how to say it.

We take the position here that writing should communicate as easily as possible. For those who are still concerned that easily communicated writing somehow lacks excellence, consider this. *It is the quality of the idea and the skill with which it is communicated that make for excellence in writing.*

There is nothing mysterious or magical about any of the suggestions listed below. They are mostly commonsense ideas that have been passed on from good writer to good writer over the years—and always influenced by readers who insist on writing that they can read.

1 Keep Focus on the Reader and the Reader's Needs

You are concerned about who will read what you have written. Of what value to your reader is what you have said? What needs do your readers have that your writing may help meet?

When you keep your writing focused on your readers you automatically solve a problem that many writers have. These writers are first concerned with solving their own problems and meeting their own needs. So they write with the intention of impressing their readers with their vast vocabulary and knowledge of the topic. They write to show off their intelligence and training in a given area. They write long and involved sentences that salve the ego of the writer but do little to aid the process of communication.

Writing with your readers in mind and focusing on their needs immediately puts a different emphasis on the writing. The writer's needs are pushed to the background, and the reader's needs are put into focus. Rather than writing to impress, the writer communicates so the reader can understand. Interestingly enough, writers who keep their readers in mind are usually those who impress their readers. Simple communication impresses. There is beauty in a complex idea expressed simply so that readers can understand it.

2 Use Active Verbs over Passive Verbs

In a seeming attempt to remain objective, and to keep themselves out of the writing, many writers avoid the active voice. The active voice is bolder, is more alive, and usually results in fewer words per sentence than the passive voice. Let's look at some examples.

The moon was jumped over by the cow. (passive—8 words)
The cow jumped over the moon. (active—6 words)

Universities are looked to by society to provide educational leadership. (passive—10 words)

Society looks to universities for educational leadership. (active—7 words)

The graduate school application was prepared by the student. (passive—9 words)

The student prepared the graduate school application. (active—7 words)

If you have difficulty knowing which is the active and which is the passive voice, remember the following sequences:

Active voice (a) Person or thing acting, (b) verb showing the action, (c) person or thing acted upon

Passive voice (a) Person or thing acted upon, (b) verb showing the action, (c) person or thing acting

3   Emphasize Nouns and Verbs

Nouns and verbs are the framework for good writing. Nouns are the foundation; verbs provide the activity. The more concrete the noun and the more active the verb, the more concise and powerful the writing. Adjectives and adverbs, often necessary to make meaning exact, should be used sparingly.

The verb should picture or imply action. Overworked verbs that have little impact include *is, are, was, were, have, has, had, went, seem,* and *get.*

The following are sentences containing weak and overworked verbs with suggestions for improvement.

Students who study generally get better grades. (Substitute *earn* for *get*.)

Air pollution is a problem for many urban residents.

Many urban residents experience air pollution problems. (Substituting the more precise and powerful verb *experience* for the weaker verb *is* and writing the sentence in the active rather than passive voice gives the sentence both more precision and more power.)

4   "Prefer the Specific to the General, the Definite to the Vague, the Concrete to the Abstract"[3]

The surest way to keep your reader interested is to write in terms of particulars and details. People want to know exactly, not generally, what is happening. They want to know about something specifically, not abstractly. Compare the following statements, the first abstract and the second concrete as to their impact:

Our family suffered economic hardship.
My husband lost his job.

There is another lesson in this guideline. For writers to write specifically, definitely, and concretely, they must know their subjects specifically, definitely, and concretely. Sometimes muddleheaded writers who don't know a subject well believe they can slip by with abstract, general writing. A good check on your preparation for writing is to ask yourself if you can write specifically and in detail about your subject. If you can't perhaps you need to spend more time researching and thinking before you begin writing.

5 Eliminate Extra Words

Many writers are wordy. A carpenter doesn't use more boards than necessary to build a house. A painter doesn't use more brushstrokes than necessary to paint a picture. An engineer doesn't use more beams than necessary to build a bridge. Likewise, a writer shouldn't use more words than necessary to communicate a message. This is not to suggest that a writer should always use exceedingly short sentences and write in a way that is stilted and choppy. What it does mean is for the writer to make every word count. Work through the following exercise and suggest one or two words to replace each phrase.

Often it is possible to cross off words and not change the meaning of sentences. For example, the words in parentheses can be eliminated without changing the meaning.

ELIMINATING EXTRA WORDS*

1 As a result of   _____
2 At the present time   _____
3 Call your attention to the fact that   _____
4 Along the line of   _____
5 Did you remember   _____
6 For the reason that   _____
7 Due to the fact that   _____
8 In advance of   _____
9 In relation to   _____
10 In the event that   _____
11 In view of the fact that   _____
12 On the subject of   _____

Answers: (1) because, (2) now, (3) remind you, (4) like, (5) forgot, (6) because, (7) because, (8) before, (9) about, (10) if, (11) since, (12) about.

* Apps, op. cit., pp. 49–50.

(absolutely) complete	by (means of)
are (as follows)	continue (on)
(at a) later (date)	during (the course of)
big (in size)	(every) now and then
blue (in color)	for (a period of) two weeks
he (is a man who)	(general) rule
(in order) to	(there are) many (who)
join (together)	(two equal) halves
later (on)	was (completely) filled
repeat (again)	(qualified) expert

6 Avoid Clichés

Use fresh language, not tired words and phrases that have lost their effectiveness because of overuse. The following words and phrases have become clichés:

As old as the hills	Not a cloud in the sky
Age before beauty	Smooth as silk
Bald as a billiard ball	Bigger and better
Last but not least	Sadder but wiser
Dark as pitch	Go hand-in-hand
Green as grass	Few and far between
Cool as a cucumber	Food for thought
You know	It goes without saying
Second to none	In this day and age
This person needs no	Leaves much to be desired
introduction	As it were

7 Explain New Words

Writers should use words they believe their readers may not know. But when they do use such words they are obligated to explain their meaning. This may be done in two ways. The word can be explained to the reader by means of a definition. Or the word can be explained by the context in which it is used. If there is any concern about confusing your reader, define the word.

For instance, assume you are writing about the process of photosynthesis: how plants form chemicals with the aid of light. You might write: "The bean plant forms carbohydrates in its chlorophyll—containing tissues, when it is exposed to light. This process is called *photosynthesis*." Or you could say, "The bean plant carries on photosynthesis—the process by which carbohydrates are formed in the plant's chlorophyll-containing tissues." In either case, the reader immediately knows the meaning of the word *photosynthesis*.

Particularly in the social sciences, ordinary words are often used as technical words. Take the word *model*. In everyday use we think of model airplanes, model cities, and fashion models. But sociologists use *model* as a technical term. The *Modern Dictionary of Sociology* defines *model* as "a pattern of relationships, either conceptual or mathematical, which is found in some way to imitate, duplicate, or analogously illustrate a pattern of relationships in one's observations of the world, such as patterns in social behavior or social structure."[4]

This dictionary then goes on to define *analogue model, causal model, conceptual model, iconic model, mathematical model, statistical model,* and *symbolic model.*

8   Vary the Length of Sentences

Readability is improved if you vary the length of your sentences. Some of them might be as long as thirty words. Others may be no longer than two or three words, maybe even one word. Variety makes for easier and more interesting reading.

9   Keep the Average Length of Sentences Short

Rudolf Flesch categorizes ease of reading based on average sentence length and average number of syllables per 100 words. He developed the following readability information as it applies to the American adult population.

AMERICAN ADULT'S READING ABILITY*

Description of style	Average sentence length	Average number of syllables per 100 words	Estimated school grades completed
Very easy	8 or fewer words	123 or less	4th
Easy	11	131	5th
Fairly easy	14	139	6th
Standard	17	147	7th or 8th
Fairly difficult	21	155	Some high school
Difficult	25	167	High school or some college
Very difficult	29 or more words	192 or more	College

* Excerpts from pp. 175, 178, and table abridged from p. 177 in *The Art of Readable Writing*, Revised Edition, by Rudolf Flesch. Copyright © 1949, 1974 by Rudolf Flesch. By permission of Harper & Row, Publishers, Inc.

Flesch's readability guidelines suggest that we should gear our writing for the high school level, or between fairly difficult and difficult, if we want to write for the average person. But Flesch points out a very important fact, "The *typical* reader for each readability level will usually be found in the *next higher* educational bracket—and sometimes the gap will even be wider."[5] This means that the reading level is one level below what we would predict from the estimated school grade completed. Sometimes the difference is even greater. So if we are writing for a college-educated audience, we should write at the high school level.

Some writers may be concerned about writing down to their audience and insulting their readers. As long as you don't write at the primer level, say, fourth or fifth grade, for a college audience, Flesch doesn't believe you'll have any problem. He says, "Your old readers will not only stay with you but you'll get more of the same kind; and they'll *read you faster, enjoy it more, understand better,* and *remember longer*."[6]

Though Flesch suggests shorter rather than longer sentences, remember that he emphasizes averages. If you plan to write at the high school level, you don't write all sentences with twenty-two or twenty-three words. Your sentences should average about that length.

10 Use Examples

When you introduce an idea, suggest an example for it. Show where the idea may be applied, where the idea fits, how the idea is related to some other idea. This guideline is related to number 4, being specific, definite, and concrete.

It is one thing to read an abstract description of an idea, but until we can read an example of the idea are we able to really understand it?

Let's use a simple illustration. Let's say you were describing a ballpoint pen to someone who had never used one. You could write: "A ballpoint pen will continue to write even when pressure is applied to the point. It's possible to make five legible carbon copies with such a pen."

The first sentence states the idea; the second is a practical application, an illustration, of the idea. You can clearly visualize what is being said.

When you use statistics it is often helpful to translate the numbers into an example that everyone can understand. If you are writing about a team of draft horses that weighs 4000 pounds, you might say the team of horses weighs as much as twenty 200-pound men.

Writing examples is a good exercise for the writer as well. Writers must clearly know the ideas they want to communicate before they can develop examples.

11 Be Positive in Statements

Most readers are disappointed to learn only what is not: they also want to learn what is. Many writers overuse the word *not*. Two problems result: first, the word *not* with its negative stance, often weakens writing, and secondly, the *not* form is often imprecise.

If we write that a person is not fat, what are we saying about the person? We know what the person is not, but we don't know what the person is. Is the person exceedingly thin? Is the person of average weight?

When we say that someone is not well, do we mean that the person is ill? If that is the case then we should say so. When we say someone is not wealthy, do we mean that he or she has average means or that the person is of low economic status?

Both these problems, weak writing and imprecise writing, can be avoided if we keep a positive approach in mind.

A PROCESS FOR WRITING PAPERS

The process described below should help improve your writing generally. But it is designed specifically to help you write such papers as themes, essays, reports, and term papers.

1 Select a Topic

You may be assigned a topic by your instructor. Or better, you may have the responsibility for selecting your own topic. Select a topic that interests you, and your writing task will be many times easier. At this stage of the writing process you may not be able to state your topic specifically. But don't be alarmed. The process is designed to help you begin with a general topic and refine it into a manageable assignment.

2 Decide on the Audience

Who is your audience? Who do you intend should read what you have written? The question may be very easily answered: your sole audience may be the instructor who has given the writing assignment. But it could be a group of students. It could be a very large audience if you are seeking to publish what you are writing. It could be a group of researchers in your field who have interest in areas similar to yours.

3 Determine Your Purpose for Writing

What purpose do you hope to accomplish with your writing? Generally, writing has three purposes or has some combination of the three: (1) to inform, (2) to persuade, or (3) to entertain. When writers inform they explain how something works, describe how something appears, tell how to make or do something, show the relationship of several factors in a complicated situation, and so on.

Writers persuade when they try to convince the reader to take a position for or against something.

Much popular writing, both fiction and nonfiction, is designed primarily to entertain. But even writing that has entertainment as its primary emphasis can also inform and/or persuade. Likewise, writing that is designed to inform or convince can also have some entertainment value.

4 Develop Questions

Raise questions that you will attempt to answer. At this early planning stage, it may be difficult to raise specific questions, but try nevertheless. As you get into the project you will want to sharpen or expand these early questions. But do write them. Questions give you a solid starting point in planning your writing. For instance, if you are writing a paper on the decline of federal support for scientific research in this country, raising questions will help you focus the topic. You might raise such obvious questions as: To what extent has federal support for science declined in the past decade? What are the causes of the decline? What is the future of science in the United States? These are starting places. They are broad questions that need refinement, but questions like these give you a place to begin.

5 Research the Topic

Using the broad questions as guides, read on the topic. Refer to Chapter 7 for guidelines on how to use the library when doing research for a paper. Check the card catalog at the library for entries on your topic. Check the *Reader's Guide to Periodical Literature* or one of several other guides to research articles, such as the *Education Index* if you are interested in topics related to education. Many college and universities now have bibliographic search systems. For a relatively small fee, a computer system will scan major computer banks around the country using key words that you give to the operator. In this way you can get in touch with the most up-to-date information on your topic that is available.

You may wish to do some original research on your topic by interviewing persons who are knowledgeable. You may have access to documents, such as letters or reports or newspaper articles, that say something about your topic.

Many student writers forget one of the most important sources of research information—themselves. You, because you have lived for 25 or 35 or 50 or more years, have experienced a great many things. Some of what you have experienced is likely related to what you are writing about. Take some time to reflect on your experience.

For all your research, whether it be library research, original research such as interviews, or reflection on your own experience, keep careful notes. Some people use elaborate card systems, while others simply keep their notes on regular-size sheets of paper. It doesn't matter what system you use as long as you use one and you use it carefully. When you copy notes from a book be sure you copy the bibliographic information for the book: author, title, publisher, publisher's city, copyright date, and page number. Many writers waste hours attempting to find for a second time material about which they have inadequate source information.

If you are copying direct quotations from books or articles, double-check to make sure they are copied accurately, including the author's punctuation marks.

You will find, as you proceed to do research on your project, that the original questions you raised will be altered. Now that you know more about the topic you can revise the questions, make them more specific, and maybe even add some that hadn't occurred to you when you first began working.

6 Develop an Outline

Outlines have little appeal for most people. Perhaps this is because in grade school many of us spent hours developing outlines for the books we were reading. But an outline, whether the highly formal one we may remember from our early education or quite an informal one, can be a valuable guide to writing.

No matter what type of paper you are writing there must be some order to it. You must present your ideas in a systematic way or your readers will not understand you.

You may present ideas in several ways. You may organize your writing around a *time sequence,* a *space sequence,* in *order of complexity from simple to complex,* in *order of importance,* or simply in terms of *major topics* that describe and explain the subject about which you are writing.

For instance, if you are writing on the development of agriculture in the United States, you could select one of several approaches for organizing the piece. If you chose to follow a time sequence, the outline might appear as follows:

Development of Agriculture in the United States

1 Colonial years
2 Pre-Civil War years

3 Post-Civil War to World War I
4 World War I to Depression
5 World War II
6 Post-World War II years to present

If a space sequence is your choice, then the outline might appear:

Development of Agriculture in the United States

1 The eastern states
2 The southern states
3 The Midwest
4 The Great Plains
5 The Far West

You could develop the subject around major topics that influenced agricultural development. Then your outline might appear as follows:

Development of Agriculture in the United States

1 Legislative influences, state and national
2 Technological innovation
3 Contributions of big business
4 Leaders in the field

How do you develop an outline? Two approaches may be followed, (1) the formal and (2) the informal.

With the formal approach, you decide on the order in which you want to present ideas as suggested above. If you plan to use a time sequence, for example, then you decide the time periods you are going to include and what supporting information you will include under each major time heading.

But what if you have problems with formal outlines? Try the informal approach. First list all the topics that relate to the questions you want to answer in your paper. Don't worry about putting them into any order, and don't be concerned about which are more important. List them one after another, not worrying about any order, sequence, or logical approach. Set the list aside for a few hours, say, overnight, then look at it again. Do you see any order to it? Is it possible to see a way of organizing the topics, say, into a time sequence or into an order of importance?

You may want to refer to Chapter 5 and the discussion of incubation as part of creative thinking. Setting aside a list of topics that apparently has no apparent order allows your subconscious to work on the problem. You will often be surprised at how an idea for ordering topics will pop into your head after or during an incubation period during which you are not consciously working on your project.

Working out an outline can be a very creative activity. But as with most creative activities, considerable work and frustration are often involved. Try several different ways of organizing the topics until you strike one that seems right, that seems to be a reasonable way of presenting your ideas.

Remember, too, that the outline is only a guide to your writing. Once you begin writing, you may discover that the outline doesn't work. Then change it. Even though you may change your outline several times during the process of writing, this doesn't negate the need for having one.

If you are not comfortable with either formal or informal outlines, you could write your paper from your research notes and not use any outline during the process. Then when you have finished writing the paper, work out an outline for it to determine if your paper does have the necessary organization to make your points.

Though this may be an attractive alternative for many students, it is usually more time-consuming. Why? Unless you have an outstanding sense of organization, following this alternative usually means considerable reorganization and rewriting of your paper.

7 Key Research Notes to Outline

Some writers number all their research notes consecutively. They include only one citation on each note card or sheet of paper. When they have finished with a draft of the outline for their paper, they key references to the research notes into the outline by simply writing in the appropriate number. This process can save much time when you are writing. You don't have to wade through a mass of research notes searching for a quotation that you vaguely remember. Also you don't risk overlooking some important piece of supporting material because you simply forgot about it.

8 Begin Writing

Up to this time you have been planning. Now it is time to sit in front of your typewriter or in front of a blank sheet of paper and begin writing.

Essentially all nonfiction writing has three parts to it—a beginning, a middle, and an end. Simple enough. The beginning tells what you are planning to say, the middle says it, and the end summarizes what you have said.

It's surprising how many writers forget those basics.

The Beginning   So how do you begin writing? You simply do it. Often the first page or two of the paper seem the most difficult to write. You want to set the tone for the piece, and you want to write an introduction that is at the same time provocative and informative. So you write a paragraph. And you tear it out of your typewriter and crumple it. You write another paragraph or two, and you toss them away. This goes on until you become so frustrated that you go out for a beer and the paper doesn't get written until another day.

One way to handle this problem is to not worry about the first couple of paragraphs or even the first couple of pages. You may in the end throw them away, but so what. Keep on writing even if you aren't particularly happy with what is coming out of your pen or your typewriter. Get it down on paper. Then you have something you work with later. You can't revise and rewrite if you have nothing to work with.

At the same time, though, don't just write phrases or words. Write complete sentences. Write in as final a form as you can, realizing that you will rewrite when necessary.

Back to the introduction. What should go into it? The purpose of the introduction—professional article writers call it the *lead*—is threefold: (1) to capture the reader's attention, (2) to supply the central idea, and (3) to lead the reader into the paper. Sometimes raising questions is a way of introducing the paper. You could use an anecdote that clearly illustrates what the main idea of the writing will be about. You could use a quotation that succinctly illustrates what is to follow.

But avoid lengthy introductions. Readers want to get on with it once their interest is aroused and they have some idea of what to expect. They want to find out what you have to say.

The Body   The middle, or body, of your paper should be relatively easy to write if you've been careful and thoughtful in developing an outline. The major headings in your outline become heads in your paper. The secondary headings in the outline become subheads. Be sure to use heads and subheads. They become visual guides for the reader, who is trying to follow the logic of your presentation. They also provide clues for readers who are scanning to determine the main ideas and perhaps decide if they should read the paper in its entirety.

Kate Turabian suggests the following approach for typing headings. This system allows for up to five ranks of subtitles. If three ranks of subtitles are required, then ranks 1 through 3 are used.[7]

Rank 1. Heading centered and underlined.
The Concept of Leisure in the United States
Rank 2. Heading centered and not underlined.
History of Leisure
Rank 3. Heading typed flush with left margin and underlined.
Leisure in Colonial Times
Rank 4. Heading typed flush with left margin and not underlined.
Ben Franklin on Leisure

Rank 5. Heading run into paragraph and underlined.
<u>Leisure and Poor Richard's Almanac</u>. Several times Franklin . . .

For those headings centered, the first and last words and all nouns, pronouns, adjectives, adverbs, and verbs are capitalized. For the remaining headings, the first word, all proper nouns, and adjectives are capitalized. Small letters are used for the remaining words in ranks 3 through 5.

Paragraphs are the building blocks for your paper. A classical way of writing a paragraph is to state your point and then illustrate or support it. You may illustrate or support through the use of examples, quotations from authorities, anecdotes, dialogue, statistics, and research data. If your paper is about solar energy, you might write:

> Even in northern states it is possible to provide a substantial amount of heat for your home with solar energy. Ole Johnson, R. R. 1, Eli, Minnesota, says, "When I put solar panels in my roof people thought I was crazy. Even my wife thought I was throwing away money. But you know in two years I've saved nearly $400 in fuel bills. No question about it, I'm sold on solar heat, even for those of us who live in the far north." Professor Clive Swenson, solar energy researcher, says, "People living in the northern United States can save up to 50 percent of their fuel bills if they use solar energy."

You first make the point about solar energy in the north. Then you use Ole Johnson's quotation and Professor Swenson's statement to support your point.

You could write your entire paper following this approach. But it is likely to become boring if you do. You may wish to begin some paragraphs with an anecdote or a quotation and end them with the topic sentence (the title given to the main point of a paragraph). Some of your paragraphs may be long; others may be only a sentence or two in length. Variation in paragraph length provides variety for the reader, just as does changing the order of ideas.

If paragraphs are the building blocks for writing, then transitions are the mortar. Transitions hold the writing together and help move the reader from paragraph to paragraph. Transitions may take several forms. Transition words such as *also, along with,* furthermore, and *especially* may be used to suggest that something is being added. Transitions may summarize with such words as *so, finally, therefore,* and *consequently.* They may be used to establish time: *now, then, afterwards, later, meanwhile, soon, frequently, never, always, occasionally.* They may link cause and effect: *because, therefore.* They may suggest that alternatives should be considered: *yet, however, but, still, nevertheless, though, whereas.* They may introduce qualification: *unless, occasionally, should, when, if.* They may refer the reader back: *they, that, he, she, it, each, many, some.*

Without transitions, writing is choppy and difficult to read. When transitions are used properly, the reader doesn't know they are there.

The Ending   The ending should tie your paper together. Rather than stop writing as you might turn off a faucet, you are obligated to provide an ending. The ending usually relates back to the introduction to your paper. You reemphasize the important points you have made in your paper or perhaps rephrase any important conclusion you have reached. As we said earlier, you summarize for your readers what you have told them.

The Title   Why wait until you have written the first draft of your paper before you write the title? Because now that you've completed the first draft you know what the article is about.

If you are writing a term paper or some other assignment for a professor, you probably wonder why to bother with a title. But if you are writing for potential publication, as many of you will likely do someday, then titles become important. On the practical level, most bibliographies list only the titles of articles or books; they don't say anything about their content. So the title must communicate the subject of the writing.

A title should be attractive and catch the reader's attention. For most purposes, the title should be concise, including as few words as possible. Many titles or academic articles are exceedingly long because the writers want to accurately communicate the subject of their papers or dissertations. Following are the titles of several academic papers: ''Adapting the Pennsylvania Extension Unit Test Demonstration Program to Limited Resource Farms: A Case Study of Seven Farms, Centre County, Pennsylvania,'' ''Motivational Orientations of Adult Educational Participants: A Factor Analytic Exploration of Houle's Typology,'' ''Criteria for Selecting a Significance Level: A Note on the Sacredness of .05,'' ''An Analysis of Selected Background Factors as Possible Predictors and Correlates of General Life Satisfaction among Young Adults from Ten Rural Wisconsin Communities.''

Usually, with some attention and concern for the problem, academic writers could write more concise titles and not fail to communicate what the paper or thesis is about.

Titles, then, should be written with three criteria in mind: (1) accuracy—the title accurately communicates what the paper is about, (2) attractiveness—the title catches the reader's eye, and (3) conciseness—the title uses a few carefully selected words to say what the paper is about.

9 Set Aside and Evaluate

When you have finished the first draft of your paper set it aside. This of course means that you cannot wait until the last minute to complete a paper assignment. When you have finished a paper, you probably believe that it is quite good and really could not be improved. But look at it again in a day or so, or even in the clear light of the next morning, and you'll be surprised at the flaws you'll spot. A few days, even a few hours, will allow you to become much more objective with your writing. On page 98 is a check sheet you can use to criticize your paper after you have allowed your writing to cool.

You may also want to give your draft paper to someone whose critical judgment you value. Try not to give it to a relative or a close friend, for it is usually difficult for these people to be critical of your writing.

10   Rewrite

Based on what you discovered when you evaluated your paper, you are now ready to rewrite it. For most writers this is a laborious and uninteresting task. Yet the work devoted to rewriting usually makes the difference between mediocre and acceptable writing. A good analogy is that of the wood-carver. A wood-carver first cuts out the shape of a wild duck. This is done with a saw and may only take a few minutes to accomplish. The bystander can see the outline of the wild duck, but everyone would agree that at this stage the work is far from completed. Next, with a skilled hand and a sharp knife the wood-carver proceeds to whittle the rough shape until the main details of the wild duck appear. Many hours are spent whittling and sanding and dressing the wood.

So it is for the writer too. The first draft of a paper, for many writers, is similar to the first cutout of the duck. The shape is evident, but much additional work is necessary. Shortening sentences, eliminating clichés, checking on the flow of ideas, and sharpening the introduction and ending are examples of what one does during the rewrite process.

For some writers one rewrite makes a final draft. But for most of us certain sections of the paper may be rewritten several times before we are satisfied with them.

SOME HELPFUL HINTS

1   Treat Sexes Equally in Writing

An important outcome of the women's movement has been the removal of sexism from writing. The present-day writer must be concerned about stereotyping males and females on the basis of their gender. And today's writer must not use the male gender to imply both sexes.

The McGraw-Hill Book Company has published a useful pamphlet that suggests many positive and practical ways for writers to eliminate sex bias from their writing. Several of the following suggestions are drawn from this source.

EVALUATING YOUR PAPER*

1 The idea is
——————— Focused
——————— Something new, or something old with a new twist
2 The purpose is clear
——————— To inform
——————— To persuade
——————— To entertain
——————— Combination of above
3 The title is
——————— Accurate
——————— Attractive
——————— Concise
4 The beginning (lead)
——————— Captures reader's attention
——————— Supplies central idea
——————— Leads reader into paper
5 The body
——————— Headings are used to set off major and minor ideas
——————— Paragraphs are building blocks
——————— Examples, statistics, anecdotes, quotations or personal experiences are used to support ideas
——————— Transitions are smooth
——————— Ideas are presented in a planned sequence
　　——————— Around a time sequence
　　——————— Around a space sequence
　　——————— From simple to complex
　　——————— In order of importance
　　——————— Major topics that describe and explain
　　——————— Other planned presentation
6 The ending
——————— Summarizes the main points of the paper
7 Composition
——————— Writing is concise
——————— Words carefully selected
——————— Cliches avoided
——————— Sentences have variety
——————— No errors in grammar, punctuation, or spelling
——————— Nouns and verbs emphasized
8 ——————— Overall feeling about paper is good

* Adapted from "Evaluating Your Article—A Check Sheet for Writers," in Jerry Apps, *Tips for Article Writers,* Wisconsin Regional Writer's Association, Madison, Wisconsin, 1973, pp. 14–15.

1 When using examples in writing, avoid job stereotyping. Women as well as men work as lawyers, doctors, truck drivers, professors, judges, bank presidents, members of congress, accountants, engineers, pilots, plumbers, and bridge-builders.

2 People of both sexes should be described as having such attributes as boldness, initiative, assertiveness, gentleness, compassion, and sensitivity. Certain characteristics should not be reserved for men and certain others reserved for women.

3 Sterotyping of the descriptions of men or women must be avoided. Do not describe women by physical attributes while describing men by mental attributes or professional position. For example, it is improper to write, "Henry Harris is a shrewd lawyer and his wife, Ann, is a striking brunette." More appropriately you might write, "The Harrises are an attractive couple. Henry is a handsome blond and Ann is a striking brunette." Or you might say, "The Harrises are highly respected in their fields. Ann is an accomplished musician and Henry is a shrewd lawyer." Or "The Harrises are an interesting couple. Henry is a shrewd lawyer and Ann is very active in community (or church or civic) affairs."

4 When describing women, avoid such terms as

the fair sex

the weaker sex

the distaff side

the girls or *the ladies* (when adult females are meant)

girl, as in, *I'll have my girl check that.*

lady used as a modifier, as in *lady lawyer*

the little woman

the better half

the ball and chain

female-gender word forms, such as *authoress, poetess, Jewess*—simply write *author, poet, Jew*

sweet young thing

co-ed (as a noun)—write *student*

Women should not be spoken about as possessions of men, but as participants in the action. Do not write, "Pioneers moved West, taking their wives and children with them." Rather, "Pioneer families moved west." Or "Pioneer men and women (or pioneer couples) moved west, taking their children with them."

5 When referring to humanity generally, the language must include women and girls. The English language has a long history of using the word *man* to refer both to the male of the species and to humanity generally. To many people, though, *man* is related more closely to maleness than to humanity. Some possible substitutions for *man*-words are as follows:

mankind: humanity, human beings, human race, people

primitive man: primitive people or peoples, primitive human beings, primitive men and women

man's achievements: human achievements

if a man drove 50 miles at 60 mph: if a person (or driver) drove . . .

the best man for the job: the best person (or candidate) for the job

man-made: artificial, synthetic, manufactured, constructed, of human origin

manpower: human power, human energy, workers, workforce

grow to manhood: grow to adulthood, grow to manhood or womanhood

6 Using a pronoun to represent both men and women presents a problem in the English language. Tradition has been to use masculine pronouns to represent both men and women. "Everyone opened *his* book." "A poet writes best when he. . . ."

Suggestions for overcoming this problem include the following:

a Reword to eliminate unnecessary gender pronouns. Rather than writing, "The average American drinks his coffee black," write, "The average American drinks black coffee."

b Rewrite using the plural. "Most Americans drink their coffee black."

c Replace the masculine pronoun with *one, you, he or she, her or his,* as appropriate. But use *he or she* variations sparingly, as they can lead to clumsy writing.

d Alternate male and female expressions and examples. "A lawyer must watch her language carefully when writing reports on her clients, as must a medical doctor when he writes reports on his patients."

7 When referring to occupations that end in *man,* replace the term with one that can refer to both men and women whenever possible:

congressman: member of Congress, representative

businessman: business executive, business manager

fireman: fire fighter

mailman: mail carrier, letter carrier

salesman: sales representative, salesperson, sales clerk

insurance man: insurance agent

statesman: leader, public servant

chairman: person presiding at (or chairing) a meeting, presiding officer, the chair, head, leader, coordinator, moderator

cameraman: camera operator

foreman: supervisor[8]

2 Follow Standard Rules for Preparing Manuscripts

Type all manuscripts double spaced, on one side of the paper, with at least 1½ inches of margin on the left side of the paper and 1 inch on the other three sides of the paper.

Use only 8½- by 11-inch white paper and black typewriter ribbon. Avoid using "erasable" paper, the kind that can be easily erased with a pencil eraser. Though this paper is handy to use, it allows the type to be easily smudged and blurred.

If you are submitting your manuscript for publication to a magazine or journal, include with the manuscript a self-addressed envelope for the return of the manuscript in the event the article isn't accepted.

Use standard footnoting and bibliographic procedures, and follow the procedures consistently throughout the manuscript. The following footnotes and bibliography are organized in the style suggested by Turabian.[9] The first example is for footnoting, the second for bibliographic entries.

When referring to a book:

1. Armand Lauffer, *The Practice of Continuing Education in the Human Services* (New York: McGraw-Hill Book Company, 1977), p. 80.

Lauffer, Armand, *The Practice of Continuing Education in the Human Services.* New York: McGraw-Hill, 1977.

When referring to an article in a journal:

1. Barbara J. Smith, "Status of Continuing Education for Librarians," *Adult Leadership* 25 (June 1977): 293.

Smith, Barbara, J. "Status of Continuing Education for Librarians." *Adult Leadership* 25 June 1977.

3 Have Available Standard References and Writer Aids

The following are some standard references for the writer:

Kate L. Turabian, *A Manual for Writers of Term Papers, Theses, and Dissertations,* 4th ed., University of Chicago Press, Chicago, 1973.

Kate L. Turabian, *Students' Guide for Writing College Papers,* 3d ed., The University of Chicago Press, Chicago, 1976.

William Strunk, Jr., and E. B. White, *The Elements of Style,* 2d ed. Macmillan, New York, 1972.

A college desk dictionary, such as *Webster's New Collegiate Dictionary*
A thesaurus

Necessary writer aids are:

Typewriter
Tape recorder—useful when collecting interview information

A quiet work place and one where you can leave your materials undisturbed when you are not working

4 Develop Techniques for Making Writing Easier

Learn how to think while you type. You will save much time if you can learn to write first drafts of your papers directly on your typewriter. Not only will you save time (once you become an accomplished typist you'll find that you can type faster and will become less fatigued while typing) you will also be able to rewrite and make corrections on the first rough typewritten copy more easily than you can on handwritten copy. Also, unless you have easily read handwriting, handwritten manuscripts are not welcomed by those you might ask to criticize your work before you begin rewriting.

When you type the first draft of your paper you can much more easily judge the length of the final draft than if you had handwritten the manuscript.

Do not be reluctant to cross out and/or throw away parts of what you have written. Though you may have labored long to develop your manuscript, and though when you've finished with the first draft you may believe the paper sparkles, develop a cross out–throw away attitude. You may toss out entire paragraphs, perhaps even entire pages, during the revision process. Painful as this may be, such pruning will improve the final product. Most persons overwrite first drafts of papers and must cut out considerable material to sharpen and generally improve their papers.

Set writing goals for yourself that are well ahead of the deadline for the paper. You might make a rule of writing three pages a day until the paper is finished, with the goal of finishing the rough draft with sufficient time for rewriting.

When taking a break from writing, stop in the middle of a sentence so that you can easily begin again after the break.

If you wish to achieve proficiency as a writer, discipline yourself to write something every day. You may wish to keep a journal as one technique for improving your writing skills. If you have achieved a certain level of proficiency as a writer and you don't write for a time, you'll find your skills decreasing. You must keep writing to keep your skills honed.

If you must write a paper with a given number of words, say, 1500 or 2000 words, you can do this without counting every word. As a rough guide, one typewritten page using pica type equals approximately 250 words. Thus a 1500-word paper would roughly equal six pages of manuscript. If you must be more precise, count all the words in ten sentences and divide by 10 to determine the average number of words per sentence.

Then count all the sentences in your paper and multiply by the average words per sentence to obtain quite an accurate word count for the paper.

If your assignment is for a long paper, say, upwards of 100 pages of manuscript, it's often useful to make folders for each of the major topics in the paper. In each folder place the research notes and other material you gather for that topic. In this way you don't have to wade through all your material while you are working on a given topic.

SUMMARY

Writing will take up much of your time as a returning student, likely second only to reading. Students are asked to write papers, themes, essays, critical reviews, research reports, and term papers. Besides these, graduate students are usually required to write theses or dissertations.

Some of the basic writing problems returning students face include a negative attitude toward writing and writing to impress.

Readability may be improved by attending to the following guidelines:

1 Keep focus on the reader and the reader's needs.
2 Use active verbs over passive verbs.
3 Emphasize nouns and verbs.
4 Be specific, definite, and concrete.
5 Eliminate extra words.
6 Avoid clichés.
7 Explain new words.
8 Vary the length of sentences.
9 Keep the average length of sentences short.
10 Use examples.
11 Be positive with statements.

A process for writing themes, essays, and term papers includes these steps:

1 Select a topic.
2 Decide on the audience.
3 Determine your purpose for writing.
4 Develop questions.
5 Research the topic.
6 Develop an outline.
7 Key research notes to outline.
8 Begin writing.
9 Set aside and evaluate.
10 Rewrite.

The following will improve both the quality and the ease with which you write:

1 Treat sexes equally.
2 Follow standard rules for preparing manuscripts.
3 Keep available standard references and writer aids.
4 Develop techniques for making writing easier.

REFERENCES

1 Edwin Newman, *Strictly Speaking: Will America Be the Death of English?* Bobbs-Merrill, Indianapolis, Ind., 1974, p. 143.
2 John Dewey, *Democracy and Education,* Macmillan, New York, 1916, 1944, pp. 216–217.
3 William Strunk, Jr., and E. B. White, *The Elements of Style,* 2d ed., Macmillan, New York, 1972, p. 15.
4 George A. Theodorson and Achilles G. Theodorson, *A Modern Dictionary of Sociology,* Crowell, New York, 1969, p. 261.
5 Rudolf Flesch, *The Art of Readable Writing,* Harper & Row, New York, 1974, p. 178
6 Ibid., p. 175.
7 Kate L. Turabian, *A Manual for Writers of Term Papers, Theses, and Dissertations,* 4th ed., The University of Chicago Press, Chicago, 1973, pp. 7 and 8.
8 *Guidelines for Equal Treatment of the Sexes in McGraw-Hill Book Company Publications,* McGraw-Hill, New York, no date.
9 Kate L. Turabian, *Students' Guide for Writing College Papers,* 3d ed., The University of Chicago Press, Chicago, 1976.

CHAPTER 5

IMPROVE YOUR THINKING ABILITY

Educational institutions teach people how to think least well of anything they do. It's one of the great contradictions of formal education.

Without question educational institutions store vast amounts of information in thousands of books, journals, theses, and research reports and in the heads of hundreds of well-trained instructors. I doubt that anyone would argue with this.

But what are you, the returning student, expected to do with all this information? Unfortunately, one popular answer to the question is that you should soak up as much information as is humanly possible in the time you have.

Soaking up facts blotter fashion is a passive process. But *thinking* is an active process. When you think, you do something. Soaking up information as it is presented to you is *not thinking*.

I sometimes share with my students the analogy of the little red wagon. Many children have little red wagons. One thing they do with their little wagons is to fill them with a variety of items—blocks, toys, and kitchen utensils, for example. Picture a little boy or girl pulling a red wagon around a living room floor and filling it with a variety of items. And picture a parent, who is playing with the youngster, asking, "Can you give me one of your blocks, please, or one of your dolls?"

The youngster reaches back to the wagon, selects the item requested, and hands it to the parent, then continues on his or her way—adding items to the wagon and disbursing them as requested.

This process of putting into, and taking from the little red wagon is not different from the process I see many students following. They listen to lectures, attend discussion sessions, read books, and constantly add information to their little red wagons without doing anything with the information.

At examination time, they reach into their red wagons and select the items called for on the exam—and often they do very well on the examinations, particularly if they've spent time loading their wagons well.

There is a vast difference between collecting facts and thinking. An overemphasis on collecting unexamined information can be one of the great deterrents to effective thinking.

This chapter is about how to improve your thinking, how to break the habit of simply accumulating information. We will explore the nature of thinking and several categories of thinking. We will examine some blocks to thinking and the conditions that enhance thinking. And we'll look at rational and creative thinking as approaches that may be followed.

THE NATURE OF THINKING

No one really knows what happens in the brain when thinking occurs. Most people agree, though, that thinking is a natural process just as eating, breathing, and observing are natural processes. Thinking is subject to errors, as are most human processes. But it is possible to learn how to improve our thinking.

Rudolf Flesch says that thinking is the manipulation of memories.[1] To say it another way, thinking is the process of making the best use of our experiences, facts, and information.

We also think with words, which are the symbols for the ideas we have in our heads. One thing we do when we think, according to Flesch, is to "detach ideas from one set of words and attach them to another."[2] In this way our thinking deals with ideas and doesn't become bound up in words. We'll say more about this later, when we explore some of the common blocks to thinking.

CATEGORIES OF THINKING[3]

One way to think about thinking is to consider the various kinds of thinking each of us does.

Daydreaming

When we are not consciously trying to direct our thinking toward some purpose, most of us engage in daydreaming. Some people refer to this process as *free association* of ideas. Generally daydreaming is centered around ourselves—what we plan to do on vacation, how well we handled some situations, etc. Daydreaming is usually considered a pleasurable experience, something that one does while waiting for the bus or while attending a boring meeting.

Defensive Thinking

Some people refer to this type of thinking as *rationalizing,* that is, finding "good" reasons for our shortcomings. Defensive thinking, however, should not be confused with rational thinking, which is discussed later. When we practice defensive thinking—and all of us do it some time or another—we seek explanations for decisions we make. We, for example, buy a car with air conditioning knowing that it reduces gas mileage, adds to the basic cost of the automobile, and has a certain amount of maintenance cost associated with it. Then we think about the reasons we can use to "defend our decision" when talking with friends. We might say that we bought air conditioning because we planned a long vacation trip through the southwestern part of the country and we could travel more miles if we kept cool. We might also say that we were surprised at how little an air conditioner adds to the basic price of a car. And we might add that an air conditioner takes much of the moisture out of the air in the car, so the atmosphere becomes both more comfortable and more healthful, especially for the children, who are bothered by high humidity.

All these reasons, though more or less true, are still examples of defensive thinking. We haven't told our friends that we've always wanted a car with air conditioning simply because we wanted it.

Defensive thinking applies not only to our actions, but also to what we believe and indeed to everything that has value because of its relationship to us. We do defensive thinking when we believe that some decision we've made, some belief we hold, some possession we've purchased may be criticized by others. And because we are human, we usually associate the criticism with criticism of ourselves as persons. The decision, the belief, the possession is an extension of ourselves, and we, through defensive thinking, set out to defend—often believing, consciously or unconsciously, that the criticism is directed against us personally. Much defensive thinking is unnecessary thinking, but nevertheless we all do it, and we must recognize its existence.

Snap Judgments

All of us, from time to time, are called upon to make decisions quickly. Do we wait and cross the street with the light, or do we dash across the street right now because no cars are coming? We must make up our minds immediately.

Life requires thousands of these snap judgments, many of them every day. Some are extremely important, while others are trivial. One of the problems with snap judgments is our ownership of the snap decision we've made. As we have more time to think, as we gather additional facts and other judgments about a matter, we may discover that the snap judgment was wrong. Given this new information we should be open to changing our earlier decision, our snap judgment, in the light of the new information that we have.

Rational Thinking

Rational thinking coupled with observation and experimentation are the basic elements of the scientific method as we know it and see it practiced throughout the world today. Later in this chapter we'll describe how to do this type of thinking.

Creative Thinking

Creative thinking is also a topic we'll discuss later in this chapter. Sometimes creative thinking is referred to as *intuitive thinking, insight development, lateral thinking* or simply *creativity.*

BLOCKS TO THINKING

Before we go on to discuss the processes of rational and creative thinking, let's look at some of the blocks to thinking. Why don't people do more rational and creative thinking?

Lack of Time

We've all heard people say, ''I don't have time to think.'' This is not an idle comment. Some people have become so busy living and making a living that they scarcely have a spare moment to breathe deeply. Thinking does require time. Though it is possible to think and do other things at the same time, usually this thinking is of the daydream or defensive type.

Herd Influence

If you have children in school you've heard again and again, ''Buy me this because everyone else has one.'' This is an example of the herd influence. We do the same thing as adults, perhaps even more so. The idea that someone should be different from the rest of the crowd is not at all accepted in our society. We have a long history of being intolerant toward the person who is a little different—the person who dresses differently, who has "strange" living habits, and so on. We have in this country what could be called "group thought." What is good for the interest of the majority of persons is good for everyone. That is the rationale for television programming, for the production of magazines, for the editing of newspapers, for the designing of clothes. The appeal is to mass thought.

Thinking, thus, can be nearly completely blocked by what the individual perceives the group to consider proper or improper. In the extreme, a person will not do anything that opposes what he or she perceives the "group thought" to be.

Multipurpose Answers

We live in a multipurpose age. Adjustable wrenches allow us to tighten several sizes of nut with one wrench. Stretch socks fit several sizes of feet, stretch caps fit any size of head, automobiles may have a back seat at one moment and, when it is dropped down, the back of the car becomes cargo space. We've carried the idea of "multipurposeness" into the world of thoughts and ideas. Do you have a problem? Here is an assortment of possible solutions to your problem. Pick out the one that comes closest to solving your problem, and use it. Keep the solutions stored in a computer, and when you have a problem, punch that information into the computer and wait for the answer to clatter out. Simple. And besides, you don't have to do any thinking. You become a searcher and a selector—and forget how to think.

Reliance on Authorities

Some students have the idea that to answer a question one need only gather information from some authority who has already dealt with the question and copy out the answer.

It appears easier to copy fifty paragraphs on what fifty "authorities" have to say about a problem or question than to think up one answer that is original. But without thinking for himself or herself a student has actually made much more work of the task.

What sometimes happens is that the student's paper becomes one huge footnote, with a few *ands* and *buts* joining it together.

The student can't be blamed totally for this nonthinking response to writing papers. Many professors are more interested in seeing how many authorities their students can cite than in finding out whether their students are able to do any original thinking in response to an assignment.

Thus students may go through school searching for authorities to quote in their papers and speeches and never once coming up with an idea or thought they can claim as their own. Occasionally a student lacks the confidence to share original ideas and hides behind the cloak of an authority.

This criticism doesn't suggest that the writings of authorities aren't important. Obviously they are. The problem is what students do with the writings of authorities.

Fear of Solitude

The best situation for thinking is being alone. But our society frowns on aloneness. We are a group-oriented society. If you are a person who prefers to spend some time by yourself, you are viewed as "different" from the norm. You are expected, in your free moments, to be doing things with others—interacting, interrelating.

This attitude of "groupness" has created in persons a fear of solitude. If it looks as if you may be alone for a time, say, a weekend, you plan your time so you are not alone or someone does it for you because he or she feels sorry that you are alone. Thus you avoid the situation that is most suitable to thinking, being alone.

Lack of Openness

The old cliché, "Don't bother me with the facts, my mind's made up," describes this situation well. A thinking person is one who is open to new ideas, to new problems, to new situations and doesn't always insist that an answer he or she has is the right one.

Words

Having an insufficient vocabulary can be a block to your thinking, for we think with words. If the symbols aren't available for the ideas that you have in your head, this can be a serious block to your thinking.

Another problem is using jargon, catch phrases, or impressive-sounding words that do not have precise meanings or may go out of fashion in a few months and then not have any meaning. Some perfectly good words, such as *relevance, operative,* and *impact,* have become jargon words and have lost their meaning and thus their utility because of over-use and imprecise use.

Another danger is divorcing a word from the idea the word represents. By repeated use over time, some words in our language—the word *democracy,* for example—have acquired assumed meanings. Mention *democracy* and most everyone will say that he or she understands what it means. But then ask three people to define it, and there is a high probability that you'll hear three different answers.

For quality thinking to occur, the person must overcome the tendency to use words that he or she doesn't know precisely. This tendency only leads to sloppy thinking, and sloppy thinking in turn results in sloppy speaking and sloppy writing.

Memorizing

Many of us have learned how to memorize quite well as a result of former formal education experiences, but few of us have learned much about how to think. Unfortunately, some people equate memorizing with thinking— no doubt as a result of these early experiences in school. Memorizing information is *not thinking*. What you do with the information once you have it in your head is what thinking is.

AIDS TO THINKING

Obviously, one major aid to thinking is overcoming the blocks listed above. But in addition to overcoming the blocks, several other factors may help you become a thinker.

Curiosity

Thinking persons are curious persons. They are constantly alert to what is going on around them. They want to know why, how, why not, and who. They are constantly questioning, constantly searching, constantly aware. They are curious about the unknown, but they are just as curious about the known. They probe and dig, question and search; sometimes with direction, sometimes without. They want to know what is going on, why it is going on, and what the alternatives are to what is going on. And at an even deeper level, they want to know what should be going on.

Willingness to Suspend Judgment

Thinking persons are willing to wait until the facts are in before they draw conclusions. And even then, when they have made up their minds, they are still open to new information and may change their minds because of this new information.

Thinking persons are willing to take time to answer questions or attempt to solve problems, making as certain as possible that they aren't prematurely leaping to a solution before they have adequately considered the question or problem itself. They are also not satisfied with the evidence and facts that are obvious to the solution of the problem or question, but search beyond the superficial for the less obvious contributions to the problem.

RATIONAL THINKING

John Dewey, an educational philosopher, wrote a small volume entitled *How We Think* in 1910, and he enlarged it in 1933.[4] This was one of the most succinct statements about the nature of rational thought that had been developed to that time, and it still serves as the basis for the many different "systems" of rational thinking that have been developed.

Dewey's process of rational thinking includes these five steps:

1 *Recognition of a difficulty*   During this first stage one recognizes that some problem exists.

2 *Definition of the difficulty*   Sometimes this step is combined with the first. It involves determining the nature of the problem, its source, its components, the factors related to it, etc., before a solution is sought.

3 *Suggestion of solutions*   Searching for alternative solutions to the problem based on the facts at hand and those obtained. Some speculation is involved.

4 *Implications of the suggestions*   Through reasoning each suggestion is analyzed to determine its implications if adopted.

5 *Conclusion*   The solution selected in step 4 is verified experimentally. The question, Does the solution solve the problem? is asked.

A Process of Rational Thinking

The following process of rational thinking, sometimes referred to as the *decision-making* or the *problem-solving process,* is based on the Dewey approach:

1 State the problem (in question form).
2 Analyze the situation.
3 Generate possible solutions.
4 Test and verify.

We'll look briefly at each step in the process, then give you an opportunity to apply the steps by working through a situation.

1   State the Problem   State the problem in the form of a question. What are you trying to find out? What do you want to know? What is the difficulty? For some persons this is the most difficult part of the entire thinking process. They face a situation and sense that something is wrong, but they are unable to ask a precise question. Until a question is asked you don't know what answer to seek.

The word *why* is often helpful to include as part of the question you are trying to formulate. The expressions *what* and *how come* are also useful.

One guideline for asking questions is to be concise. State as specifically as possible what question or questions are inherent in a problem situation.

Consider the following situation. You are a corporate executive and are reviewing your firm's gross revenues for a 5-year period: 1973–$45 million, 1974–$68 million, 1975–$106 million, 1976–$156 million, 1977–$165 million. What question or questions might you ask after reviewing these figures? Each year the gain in gross revenue has been about 50 percent over the previous year, except in 1977. If 1977 were comparable to the other 4 years, you would expect the gross revenues to be well over $200 million. The obvious question is, Why did the upward trend of revenues fall off in 1977? As the corporate executive, you can't deal with your firm's problem until you have asked the question.

2 Analyze the Situation Once you've stated the question, you must find out as much as you can about the situation. What are the facts? Using the example of the corporation executive above, you might ask: What was the nature of the economy during 1977? What problems are we having in the firm that may have had an effect on sales? Was the dropoff in sales evident throughout the year, or was it more of a problem in one of the quarters than in the others? The question to ask in analyzing a situation may be helped with such expressions as *what, where,* and *to what extent.*

An analysis of the situation also includes determining sources of help in solving the problem. Don Koberg and Jim Bagnall suggest the following as basic questions that help in finding resources:

Where is information available on this question?
Who could help me answer the question?
What work has already been done in attempting to answer this question?
Are books or other references available that may help me?
What resources do I have available to me now that will help answer this question?[5]

In analyzing a situation you search for specific information. And you are not enticed with skipping immediately to some solution, some answer to your question. You force yourself to obtain as much information as possible about a situation, and you withhold judgment until you are satisfied that you've carefully and precisely analyzed the situation.

3 Generate Possible Solutions Once you've stated the question and analyzed the situation, you are ready to look for possible answers to the question. Again, you must avoid the tendency to accept the first solution or answer that sounds promising.

This step of the process can be quite creative. Force yourself to identify possible solutions beyond those that look plausible at first glance. Utilize the various resources that are available to you. But be cautious of accepting ready-made answers out of hand. If someone else has worked on a similar problem, and the answer to the problem sounds as if it would work in your situation, determine *how* similar the situation was to yours. Are your situation and the situation you read about sufficiently similar so that you can seriously consider the answer? If so by all means accept it; there is no sense in "reinventing the wheel."

But do not accept the answer without testing it in your situation, which leads us to the discussion of the next step.

4 Test and Verify Once suggested solutions to your problem have been generated, you must test and verify them to find out if they work, if they answer the question you raised in step 1. What you have been doing during this entire process is searching for a cause for something or the explanation for a situation. You are trying to answer a *why, what,* or *how come,* question. You don't really know which of your suggested answers is correct until you try them.

Let's refer back to the example of the business executive with declining profits. This person could have suggested that profits declined during 1977 because of a sluggish economy. To check the accuracy of this answer, the executive could have consulted the gross profit figures for similar business, the stock market history during the past year, and so on. This information would either help confirm or help deny the answer the executive had suggested.

Let's now move to a practical example that requires rational thinking.

RATIONAL THINKING*

A fire had swept through a vast section of forest, and a ranger had rapidly assembled twenty-seven volunteer fire fighters. He divided them into groups and, working quickly, gave each group a two-way radio.

"A helicopter will patrol the area," he announced. "If you get in trouble, radio the 'copter and it will pick you up." Then each team was instructed in the use of the radio.

Later, when the fire was extinguished, one of the groups (consisting of three men) was missing. After a two-day search, their charred remains were found in a valley.

RATIONAL THINKING* (*Cont.*)

1 *Statement of the problem* (*in question form*) Write a question (questions) that will focus on the problem in this situation.

_____

_____

_____

Answer. Examples of questions you might have written are, Why weren't the men rescued? and What killed these men? It is premature to ask, How can these deaths be prevented in the future? What must be established first is what the problem is—what the question is that must be answered.

2 *Analyze the situation* Go back and read the incident again. In step 1, the problem was pinpointed with the question, Why weren't the men rescued? Now the ranger must analyze the situation. Write at least four questions the ranger might ask to learn more about this situation.

_____

_____

_____

_____

Answer Good questions to ask are the following:
Where, when, and by whom were the men last seen?
Did the helicopter crew receive a call from the men?
Was this the only failure of the rescue plan, or were there other, more minor failures?
Where and in what condition were the remains of the men (and of the radio) when found?
Have there been similar failures of the rescue plan in the past?
The following are not appropriate questions to ask at this time because they attempt to get at the cause of the problem. They should be reserved for step 3.
Did the radio fail to work properly?
Did the men panic and forget how to operate the radio?
Did the heat from the fire damage the radio?

3 *Generate possible solutions* Once you have identified the problem and have gathered all the pertinent facts about the case (analyzed the situation), you are ready to look for possible reasons for why the men weren't rescued. Before the ranger can learn how to prevent future accidents of this type, he must search out the cause.
When the ranger analyzed the situation he learned the following:
The helicopter crew said that they had not received a call from the three men.
The men had last been seen walking over the crest of a hill, into the valley in which their remains were later found.
The metallic remains of the radio were found next to the remains of the men.
Another group of fire fighters, trapped on a knoll by encircling flames, had radioed the helicopter and were rescued.
None of the other fire fighters needed rescuing.
During another fire, 9 months earlier, a team of fire fighters had died in the flames; the helicopter had reported receiving no call for help; the remains were found in a dry streambed between two hills.

RATIONAL THINKING* (*Cont.*)

Write at least two possible causes for the failure of the rescue plan.

_____

_____

Answer.   Here are examples of five possible reasons why the men weren't rescued:

The men did not know how to operate the radio properly.

The members of the helicopter crew *did* receive a call for help, but they said they didn't in order to hide their failure to rescue the men.

The radio signal was cut off by the crest of the hill and was never picked up by the helicopter's receiver.

The radio was defective, possibly affected by the heat.

The men panicked and were unable to radio for help.

4 *Test and verify*   Now you must determine which of the possible solutions is most apt to be the right one.

First compare each suggested solution with the facts generated during step 2, analyze the situation. Which of the five suggested solutions listed above is the most likely to be correct? Circle its number below.

$$1 \quad 2 \quad 3 \quad 4 \quad 5$$

Also, in a sentence or two, suggest a method that may be used to verify the solution you suggested, to determine if it is the correct one.

_____

_____

Answer.   The most likely solution is 3, "The radio signal was cut off by the crest of the hill and was never picked up by the helicopter's receiver." It fits all the facts: that no call for help was received, that the radio was found near the remains of the man, and that in the other incident, 9 months ago, the men perished in a similar location—between two hills. The other four suggested solutions are not as likely, for the following reasons:

"The men did not know how to operate the radio properly." Although this solution cannot be ruled out entirely, it does seem unlikely. The men were instructed in the use of the radio.

"The members of the helicopter crew *did* receive a call for help, but they said they didn't in order to hide their failure to rescue the men." No evidence has been presented to indicate that the crew tried to rescue the men.

"The radio was defective, possibly affected by the heat." Although possible, this is unlikely. How does it explain the fact that the two failures occurred in similar physical environments?

"The men panicked and were unable to radio for help." This is mere speculation. The facts do not point to it as a likely cause. It could be true, but many assumptions are required.

The most distinctive fact is that the two tragedies occurred in similar terrain, in a valley or depression. The only suggested solution that grows out of this distinction is 3. Of course it may not be correct. How do you find out? You attempt to verify it, to check it out in the field.

Here are two procedures that the ranger might follow to verify, to determine if his suggested solution is the correct one.

RATIONAL THINKING* (*Cont.*)

Station a person with a radio in the location where the three men died, have a helicopter patrol overhead, and see if and where the signal is cut off.
Establish the location of the helicopter at the time the men would have tried to radio it. Do this by autopsy (establishing probable time of death), by finding out the time at which the men were last seen, etc., and by questioning the crew and fire fighters as to the location of the helicopter at that time. In other words, find out if the helicopter was in a position where a signal from the men would have been cut off by the crest of the hill.

In summary, rational thinking is a systematic way of answering questions and dealing with problems. The process involves a careful attention to each of the four steps: (1) statement of the problem (in question form), (2) analysis of the situation, (3) generation of possible solutions, and (4) testing and verification. You do not move on to another step until the step you are dealing with is properly carried out.

A difficulty faced by many people is to hurriedly jump to step 3, searching for solutions and answers, before carefully defining the problem and learning all the facts about it.

*Adapted from Richard W. Samson, *Problem Solving Improvement*, McGraw-Hill, New York, 1970, pp. 26–41. Used with permission of McGraw-Hill Book Company.

CREATIVE THINKING

At the beginning of this chapter we said that thinking was the process of making the best use of our experiences, facts, and information. Creative thinking takes this definition a step further. *Creative thinking is a process that brings something new into being.*

As we outlined above, the process of rational thinking has definite steps, with definite activities that must be carried out at each step for the process to move forward.

Creative thinking is best described as having phases rather than steps. These phases often overlap with each other. And activities carried out within each phase are not so clearly defined as in rational thinking. In fact, as you study the phases, you'll notice that one of the phases suggests that no activity at all takes place.

A number of descriptions of how creative thinking may take place are offered in the literature. One of the early writers in the field of creative thinking was Graham Wallas.

Wallas suggested the following phases for creative thinking, which he referred to as "stages of thought":

Preparation   Illumination
Incubation   Verification[6]

Preparation

During this phase of creative thinking you state as clearly as possible the question you want answered. And you learn as much about the problem situation as you can. It is more than studying a situation to learn the facts about it; it is more than succinctly stating the problem in question form—although this is a very important part of the phase.

This phase of creative thinking includes what Rollo May describes as an "encounter"[7] and what Jerome Brunner calls "freedom to be dominated by the object."[8]

Preparation means total involvement with the problem situation. You learn all the facts of the situation to be sure. And you force yourself to put off searching for easy answers to the question you have raised. But more than that, you become emotionally involved with the question. You search for its essence. You look at it from every angle you can think of. You look behind it; you look at it from the side, from the top, from the bottom, and from several feet away. You concentrate on the question intensely, giving your entire time and energy to it. You search for information about the problem and accept it even though at the instant it seems to bear no relationship to the question you are attempting to answer. You write down information you've collected about the question, but you don't worry about organizing it or categorizing it. You simply record it.

You talk to others about the question, gathering what information and opinions they may have. And you record this information, again not worrying about where it fits.

You read, you listen, you record.

Having the question clearly stated is important, even though during this phase you may find it necessary to restate the question several times. Nevertheless, the question carefully stated is your guide to collecting information—your guide for the encounter with the situation.

Incubation

Leave the problem or question. Take a walk. Go sit out on the back porch. Walk down to the drugstore. And do not think about the problem or question you've just recently spent so much time with.

During this phase of creative thinking try to do something entirely different from what you had been doing. To use a cliché, take your mind off your problem.

"How can anything happen if I don't work on it?" and "Am I not wasting valuable time if I leave the problem I've been working on before I've come up with any answers?" you may ask.

The experiences of people who have practiced creative thinking, particularly the incubation phase, are these. Leaving the problem and doing something quite different, whether it be physical activity, such as playing tennis, or relaxation allows the unconscious to take over and work on your problem.

We are not talking about something that is mystical or supernatural, but about that part of our makeup that the psychologists refer to as the *unconscious*. Our dreams, of course, are one product of our unconscious. But the unconscious can also serve to us to help sort out and make sense of the mass of information we've fed into it during the preparation phase described above.

Research is beginning to uncover how the unconscious works. But no one really knows what to expect from its work. That, of course, is at the same time exciting and depressing. We take what we get from the unconscious, which sometimes may be nothing and at other times may be a profound answer to our question or a most creative solution to our problem.

What happens when the unconscious is at work is the most creative part of creative thinking, for the unconscious often comes up with never-before-thought-about combinations of ideas.

The unconscious does need an opportunity to function. If we are so intent on constantly working at our thinking, without any time for recreation or relaxation, then we are not allowing one of our built-in resources to work.

Some people find that the moment just before they go to sleep, the transition time from conscious to unconscious, is the time when many of their most creative ideas pop into their heads. If this happens to you, take advantage of it. Keep a notebook by your bed and jot down the ideas when they flash into your head.

Illumination

When an "insight," the product of incubation, pops into your head, you have reached the illumination phase of creative thinking.

When an insight breaks through into our consciousness, we almost always recognize it as the "right" answer to our question or the "right" solution to our problem. Even though we have no rational basis (how could we have a rational basis when we weren't doing rational thinking?) we know the answer is the right one. We also are usually impressed with the simplicity of the answer. A usual response that some people make is, "Why didn't I think of that before?" We know the answer is right, but we have no way of proving it. We don't know the source of the idea, other than it came from the mass of information that we fed into our heads, which interacted with the years of experience we've gained through living.

Usually the moment when the insight strikes is a joyous moment for us emotionally. We are struck with wonder and astonishment that after all of the work we've put in on a question the answer should be so simple and straightforward.

Verification

We try out our insight and see if it indeed does solve our problem or answer our question.

A Personal Experience

Let me share a personal example of creative thinking to illustrate the process. When I was 12 years old I'd saved enough money to purchase a speedometer for my bike. Upon opening the box that contained the speedometer I noticed that one of the nuts that was to fasten the speedometer to the bike was missing. I soon was able to define my problem: How was I to fasten the speedometer to the bike without the nut?

I searched the box again and again to see if I had overlooked the nut. It was not there. At that time in my life I wasn't aware of any processes for problem solving. But I was aware that unless I got another nut I couldn't use my new speedometer. What were the alternatives? They seemed obvious: The first was to wait until the next time my father could take me to the store—it would be at least another week, and there was a good chance they didn't have another speedometer but would have to order one. A second alternative was to try to find a nut like the missing one on my father's workbench.

I searched and searched, using the picture from the direction sheet as a guide. But no nut even remotely like the needed one was on or around my father's workbench.

I sat on the grass and read the directions again. I looked carefully at all the pieces that were in the box. I assembled the parts, except that I couldn't fasten the speedometer to the bike because the nut was missing.

I reluctantly left my problem to eat supper and then worked on it again until it was time for bed. I'd given up hope by that time and was sure I'd have to wait until we went to the store again before I could solve my problem.

When I was lying in bed, not thinking at all about my bike or my new speedometer, the answer came to me. What I must do is wind some friction tape around the mounting brace, and then I could use the nut that fastened the speedometer cable to the speedometer to also hold the speedometer in place.

I pulled on my clothes, raced down the stairs, and found some friction tape. In 15 minutes I had the new speedometer securely fastened to my bike and my problem solved. I didn't need the missing nut after all.

Now let's go back and see where the various phases of creative thinking fit the example. Up until the time I got ready for bed I was in the preparation phase—carefully defining the problem, learning as much as I could about what I had to work with, studying the situation as thoroughly as possible, and being committed to finding an answer that didn't require waiting at least a week.

Incubation occurred during the time I got ready for bed and just before I went to sleep.

Illumination was when the insight popped into my head, seemingly from nowhere. In fact the friction tape idea surprised me because I had not once that afternoon even considered friction tape as something that might be useful in solving my problem. I had, however, often used friction tape as I'd worked with my father on other projects.

Verification came when I tried out the idea and found that it worked well.

Blocks to Creative Thinking

One of the most pervasive blocks to creative thinking is an assumption that many people have that one should be able to communicate exactly how one arrived at an answer or solution to a problem. Because they can't communicate how the answer was obtained, many people avoid paying attention to their insights and discount them as nonrational.

Insights *are* nonrational; that's why they are insights. But our society by and large is a rational society and tends to use rational thought as the basis for comparison.

Of course artists—poets, novelists, painters, musicians, etc.—use creative thinking to come up with their ideas.

But our society tends to separate the artist from the scientist, tends to separate creative thought from rational thought. Not only does our society separate artists from scientists, but it also makes a strong claim that what scientists do is more important than what artists do. If you don't believe this reflect on the amount of tax money used to support scientists versus the tax money used to support artists.

Other blocks to creative thought are the following:

1 Fear of being an individual, of being different from other people. If you come up with a new idea you will be different.

2 Fear of being thought a fool. People who have new ideas have been thought fools for all time. The Wright Brothers, Einstein, Edison, and Ford at one time were thought foolish.

3 Fear of making a mistake. If you must always be right, then creative thinking is not for you; indeed, rational thinking may cause you to make mistakes too.

When Creative Thinking Is Most Useful

Although it is possible to often blend together rational and creative thinking, there are occasions when you may wish to do only creative thinking.

1 When attempting to create new ideas. If you are interested in finding new ways of organizing things, new approaches to looking at things, new ways of communicating ideas to others, fresh ways that haven't been considered before, try creative thinking.

2 When attempting to solve certain types of problems. Edward de Bono says that there are three types of problems: (a) a problem that requires new information or improved techniques for handling information to solve it, (b) one that requires no new information but requires a new way of rearranging the information that is there, and (c) one that is initially viewed as no problem. The third type of problem refers to the situation in which one is satisfied with the present situation to the point of not being able to see any problem in it. The problem, therefore, is to realize that a problem exists.

The first type of problem may be solved by following conventional rational thinking processes of the type outlined earlier in this chapter. The second and third types of problems require creative thinking for their solution.[9]

3 When taking stock of what already exists (a challenge of the ordinary). Creative thinking can help you look critically at those ideas, theories, approaches, that one takes for granted and doesn't question. This type of thinking will help you challenge assumptions that people may have accepted for years. The idea is not to challenge existing ideas, theories, etc., with a mind to changing them, although change may result, but to assess these things because they exist and haven't been assessed for a long time. Creative thinking may be used to constantly look at old things in an attempt to find a new way, even though the old way may stand as the better way at the moment.

Rational Thinking and Creative Thinking Compared

As we've explained above, rational thinking is sequential; that is, there is a series of steps to be followed. Creative thinking does not rigidly adhere to steps to be followed.

The solution to a problem arrived at by rational thinking and the process you used in arriving at the solution can be quite easily communicated to another person. Indeed, another person could quite easily follow the same steps you did, and if he or she followed them correctly the chances are quite high that the other person would arrive at the same answer you did.

The person doing creative thinking will often arrive at an answer or solution but not be able to explain how he or she did it. Thus the process cannot be repeated in the same way by someone else.

When doing rational thinking one concentrates on excluding what is irrelevant to the process. When doing creative thinking, one does not make judgments about what is and what is not irrelevant but considers, indeed welcomes, all information.

Though the two approaches to thinking are considerably different from one another, one is not better than the other. The two approaches may be used to complement each other. Creative thinking may generate ideas and approaches that rational thinking may later develop and test and verify. Creative thinking, when incorporated into the rational thinking process—particularly at the stage of generating solutions—enhances the rational thinking process by providing more alternatives to select from.

SUMMARY

Thinking is not taught often. Students become knowledge blotters, soaking up the knowledge provided by authorities.

Thinking is, however, a natural process for all of us, as natural as breathing, eating, or observing. We all daydream, do defensive thinking, and make snap judgments.

We also have the ability to do both rational and creative thinking, and we can improve these two thinking processes.

Some blocks to thinking include lack of time, herd influence (''be like the crowd''), multipurpose answers, reliance on authorities, fear of solitude, lack of openness, insufficient vocabulary, and a confusion of memorizing with thinking.

Our ability to think is enhanced by attitudes of curiosity and willingness to suspend judgment.

A process for rational thinking includes (1) statement of problem, (2) analysis of the situation, (3) generation of possible solutions, (4) testing and verification.

A process for creative thinking includes the phases of (1) preparation, (2) incubation, (3) illumination, and (4) verification.

Often creative thinking is inhibited because (1) we cannot communicate the process we used for arriving at insights; (2) many people assume that rational thought is more important than creative thought; (3) we fear being an individual, separated from the group; (4) we fear being thought a fool; and (5) we fear making a mistake.

Creative thinking is most useful when we want to create new ideas, solve problems when rational thinking doesn't fit, and challenge what already exists but is seldom, if ever, questioned.

REFERENCES

1 Rudolf Flesch, *The Art of Clear Thinking,* Harper & Row, New York, 1951, p. 8.
2 Ibid., p. 49.
3 M. E. Bennett, *College and Life: Problems of Self-Discovery and Self-Direction,* McGraw-Hill, New York, 1952, pp. 172–177.
4 John Dewey, *How We Think,* Heath, Boston, 1933.
5 Don Kobert and Jim Bagnall, *The Universal Traveler,* William Kaufmann, Inc., Los Altos, Calif., 1974, p. 48.
6 Graham Wallas, *The Art of Thought,* Harcourt, New York, 1926, pp. 80–81.
7 Rollo May, *The Courage to Create,* Norton, New York, 1975, p. 41.
8 Jerome S. Bruner, *On Knowing,* Atheneum, New York, 1973, pp. 25–26.
9 Edward de Bono, *Lateral Thinking: Creativity Step by Step,* Harper and Row, New York, 1973, p. 58.

CHAPTER 6

BUILD YOUR VOCABULARY

One of the first things you'll notice when you return to school is the abundance of words. Words rain down upon you from the podiums of the lecture halls. They cover the pages of the many books, journals, monographs, and magazines you pore over. They echo down the halls of the college and university buildings as students and professors talk to each other.

Words will engulf you at every turn when you return to school. They will become your daily companions whether you wish it or not, for the business of college and university life is carried out with words.

When you return to school, you'll discover that many of the words you read and hear are old friends. These are the words you learned to know and use many years ago, and you are quite comfortable with them.

You will also discover many words that are acquaintances; that is, you believe you understand what they mean but you seldom, if ever, speak or write them.

You'll also be surprised that some of the words you have used over the years and considered old friends because you understood their meanings are now used in different ways, with different meanings. For example, when you heard the word *society* you always related it to such things as the society pages in the newspapers, where those people who were considered more well-to-do had their various parties, marriages, and the like reported. But you discover quickly that the social sciences use the word *society* differently. Within the social sciences, it is defined as a group of people who have a common and at least somewhat distinct culture and have a feeling of unity toward each other. You discover that the word *society* has a more precise meaning in an academic setting.

And depending on your area of academic interest, you'll likely meet face to face a plethora of words you've never met before; never, ever, heard of. To add to the discomfort of meeting these never-before-met words, you discover that the students around you—those taking classes with you—seem to know these words and toss them around as if they've known them since first grade.

A fundamental skill, then, is to devise a system for learning new words, a process or procedure that will make you comfortable with those strange-sounding words you are meeting for the first time.

CLASSIFICATIONS OF WORDS

Before we discuss some of the approaches you might use to become acquainted with new words and improve your vocabulary, let's look at two ways words may be classified: (1) degree of formality and (2) way they are used.

Degree of Formality

Porter Perrin suggested that we can classify words into three levels of formality: (1) vulgate, (2) informal, and (3) formal.[1]

1 *Vulgate,* which means *in general circulation,* refers to those words that are used in everyday language. These are the words we use when we talk to our families and friends; when we discuss what is going on in the world during coffee break; when we tell stories; when we carry on everyday, ordinary conversations with people. Vulgate words are mostly spoken words. There is variation among these words as you travel around the country, both in the ways the words are pronounced and in the different words used to describe the same thing.

Vulgate words also include the slang words of the day, those words that sound so good and are so fun to say that we say them to death and then they depart and are replaced with new slang words.

2 Informal words are those that are both spoken and written. These include the words that are used in letters we write to friends and in a journal we may keep to record our inner thoughts and the daily weather. These are also the words we read in most newspaper stories, hear on television, and read in magazines and books on general subjects. These are the words we hear at a public lecture and read in a novel. Informal English is used in essays, in much poetry, and in most business writing.

3 Formal words, though used less frequently in everyday life, are used a great deal in colleges and universities. Most of the scientific and technical writing that is written on special subjects for professional audiences falls into the category of formal English. Many textbooks are written in formal English. Most reference books, nearly all theses and dissertations, and most college term papers, too, are in formal English.

Formal words are precise words, used to describe an event or activity with such precision that there is no mistaking what is being described. For example, *median* is a formal word. Used in mathematics and particularly in statistics, it defines the middle value in a series of mathematical values and serves to divide the series in half. The word *average* is an informal word that is commonly used in our language to describe a central tendency. But for technical purposes the word *average* is not precise enough, for there is more than one type of average. *Median* is one type. Other types of averages are *mean* and *mode*.

Another category of formal words that must be mentioned because you'll likely meet them are words that can be described as pretentious. Occasionally both students and professors attempt to make simple matters unnecessarily complicated by using polysyllabic words to describe a situation when a monosyllabic word would do the job as easily and certainly more directly.

Edwin Newman, mentioned in Chapter 4, comes down hard on the social science community which he believes works at trying to make clear ideas opaque. In many ways Newman is right, for you, too, will discover, if you take any courses in the social sciences, that some social science professors pride themselves on attempting to make things complicated when they really aren't. For example, rather than saying that someone is *speaking,* they say the person is *articulating.* When two people are talking to each other they are having a *dialogue.* It's obviously not academic enough (at least in the minds of some professors) that two people conversing can be simply *talking* to each other.

The same goes for thinking. To many social scientists the word *thinking* is replaced with *conceptualization.* Apparently people in academic circles cannot be expected to only think, for that must be a task that everyone can do. Conceptualization sounds as if it is reserved for a limited number of persons who somehow think differently, think more deeply, or at least think more often. Other examples are *utilize* for *use* and *methodology* instead of method.

One of the difficult tasks is to sort out the words that are truly technical and precise and are used to describe an event or object that no other word or words can adequately describe, and those words that are pretentious and used to impress—and usually confuse rather than enlighten the reader.

Way They Are Used

How are words used? The answer seems obvious. We use words in speaking and in writing: in communicating to others something we have to say, some idea we have, some belief we hold.

But we also use words in thinking. When we think, there is no magical process taking place in our heads that rearranges some mystical fluff and makes our thoughts out of all that. When we think, we think in words. We rearrange words in our heads, pushing new ones together, putting old ones together with new ones, and rearranging old ones. When we are thinking we are thinking with words. Words are the tools of our thinking, the symbols of our thoughts. Without them our thinking about ideas is impossible.

From this line of reasoning, it seems logical to accept the idea that the more carefully we develop our vocabulary, the more careful will be our thinking. As we know words precisely, we are able to think precisely.

Of course the three uses I've mentioned are all related to each other. We think the same words we write and speak. That is not to say that our spoken language and our writing language are identical. They usually are not. We write words that we are uncomfortable speaking, and we may arrange our written sentences in ways different from the ways we arrange our spoken sentences. But nevertheless, the words we are writing or speaking are the words we are thinking.

We must also point out that having a substantial vocabulary of words that you can precisely define and are comfortable to use in written or spoken form doesn't automatically ensure that the quality of thinking, the profoundness of your thoughts, will improve.

We must remember that words are tools. They assist you in building and understanding ideas, but they do not replace ideas. For example, carpenters use a great many tools. They must know how to use saws, hammers, squares, and so on. The more tools they know how to use, the better the chances that they will be able to build fine houses. If carpenters knew only how to use hammers and saws, they would be severely limited in house building. But just because a carpenter knows how to use many tools doesn't automatically mean that the quality of the carpenter's house building will improve. The chances are that it should, but whether or not the house building is of high quality depends on how the carpenter uses the tools.

So it is with the person using words. Some persons with vocabularies well above average seldom come up with ideas that have merit. Occasionally, the person with a less than average vocabulary is able to develop an idea that is truly profound and is a breakthrough in thinking.

But by and large, the more tools you have and the more ability you have in using them, the more apt you are to do good thinking.

We've all had experiences in dealing with people who've expressed concern about their ability to communicate. I worked with a student who was returning to college after more than 10 years away from formal learning. One day we sat down to discuss a paper she had written for one of her courses, on which she'd received an unacceptable grade. After some minutes of discussion, she got to the heart of the problem when she said, "I knew what I wanted to say, but I just couldn't find the words to say it."

Her inadequate vocabulary proved to be one of her most serious problems in adjusting to college.

NUMBERS OF WORDS

We are all aware of the explosion of new ideas in our world today. People talk about how the amount of known information in the world is increasing at such rates that the world we knew as children is an entirely different world when we become adults.

Such is also the case with words. The number of new words in the English language is constantly increasing. It is estimated that Samuel Johnson's dictionary of 1755 contained about 15,000 words. Today's unabridged dictionaries contain upwards of ½ million words, with the number increasing in each new edition. Today's desk dictionaries contain about 150,000 words.

It is estimated that the average person knows and uses between 5000 and 10,000 of all these words. A so-called educated person, someone with some college education, may be familiar with the meanings of 20,000 to 50,000 words. This doesn't mean that the college-trained person uses all these words, though.

LEARNING NEW WORDS

Let's begin by assuming that you as a returning student are interested in learning new words. In a sense you have little choice, for new words will meet you in every course you take, particularly if you are studying in areas that are new to you. What approaches can you use in adding to your vocabulary?

Study Vocabulary Books

On the market today are a number of books designed to improve your vocabulary. They are all do-it-yourself in their approaches and claim that you will be able to improve your supply of usable words by large numbers and in a short time. The books are generally easy to read and in some instances even quite entertaining. But by and large they are not going to help you learn the words you need to know to become a successful return-ing student. On the negative side, what may happen is that you may accumulate a collection of words that simply don't fit the kind of life you live and the kind of academic situation in which you study. In a sense your newly acquired vocabulary of quickly learned words becomes so much excess baggage. You've invested time and energy that could have been better used doing other things.

Read Books

Some people suggest that the best way to improve your vocabulary is by reading "good" books, particularly books that contain words you don't know. This system would work if you would stop to look up the words you don't know in a dictionary. But you won't learn new words automat-ically by just reading them, not very often anyway. Occasionally, as you'll see later, it is possible to derive the meaning of words from their context. But this process, too, must be supplemented with dictionary work.

Increase Vocabulary Through Natural Growth

By living, listening, and associating with people you'll be able to increase your vocabulary, is what this approach suggests. Obviously this is true for the young child who is just getting acquainted with the language. But for the adult, there are many times when the opposite is true. That is, the number of words known can actually decrease with time if the words are not used. So we can't depend on natural growth to increase our vo-cabularies.

Make a Word List

Some persons suggest that the simplest way to increase your word power is to go to the dictionary, pull out five or six words that you don't know, write them and their definitions on a card, and then, in off moments during the day, study the card. As we'll see later the idea of using a card is not bad. But to pick any five or six words from the dictionary will often leave you with a collection of words you can't use.

Study the Dictionary

Granted, a great deal can be learned from studying the dictionary. And of course you can also learn a great deal from studying the phone book. The problem with "studying the dictionary" is no different from that associated with making word lists and studying vocabulary self-help books: you end up with words that don't fit anyplace. What is different about studying the dictionary compared with some of the other approaches we've mentioned is that dictionary studying is about the most boring thing I can think of doing. I'll quickly add that used as it should be used—to find out something about a word you don't know—the dictionary can be one of the most exciting books on your shelf. It's all in how you use it.

Become a Word Sleuth

A more positive way of increasing your collection of useful words is a process that I call *becoming a word sleuth*. Becoming a word sleuth starts with the assumption that you are interested in words and in increasing the number of words you can effectively use.

INTEREST IN WORDS

As we've mentioned above, words are symbols and we use them as tools. But they also have histories that make them more than abstract symbols that are useful only for communication. If we are truly interested in words, we will find some most interesting information as we dig into their histories.

For example, many words in our English language come from the names of people. The *leotard,* which means *a close-fitting garment usually with long sleeves, a high neck, and ankle-length legs,* is named after Jules Leotard. Jules Leotard was a French aerialist in the nineteenth century, and he perfected an aerial sommersault that thrilled circus audiences of the day. But he was remembered for the costume he wore, not the feats he performed.

Rudolph Diesel was a German who invented a special type of engine that bears his name.

And it is claimed that on August 6, 1762, John Montague, the Fourth Earl of Sandwich, ordered cold, thick-sliced beef to be placed between two pieces of toasted bread. Thus was born the sandwich.[2]

One fascinating place to start if you are interested in ferreting out the histories of words is the *Oxford English Dictionary*[3] (OED), which comes in thirteen volumes plus supplements. For example, if we go to the *Oxford English Dictionary* with the word *book,* we discover that the word comes from the old Teutonic word *bok-s,* which means *a writing tablet, leaf,* or *sheet.*

The OED further explains that some people associate the word *book* with the beech tree, which comes from the old English *boc.* Some persons suggest the first books were made of beechen tablets or that words were cut in the bark of beech trees. OED questions this genesis for the word *book*, however. All of that and much more you can learn about the word *book* from the *Oxford English Dictionary*.

I was curious about the history of the word graffiti, which refers to those words and drawings that grace the walls of subways, elevators, and rest rooms throughout the country. The OED says that the word comes from the Italian word *graffito*, which means *to scratch*. Makes sense.

The history of the word *college* intrigued me. The word, according to the Oxford English Dictionary, comes from the Latin word *collegium*, which means *a partnership, a colleagueship*, hence *a body of colleagues*.

Other college-related words that intrigued me were *commencement* and *faculty*. *Commencement* should not be applied to the granting of a diploma. The word comes from the practice, in medieval universities, of requiring graduates to spend some time teaching beginners. When one finished formal studies at the university, one commenced to teach those who were just beginning their academic work.

Faculty comes from the Latin *power* or *ability*. It refers to the capacity to do something and is sometimes used when referring to people who are fully competent. We say they have *all of their faculties*.[4]

Another interesting way of studying the history of words is to associate words we use today with the ethnic groups that brought them to this country or with the American Indians who used the words before our ancestors arrived.

Some of the words we've borrowed from the American Indians include *sequoia, squash, tamarack* (a tree), *chipmunk, moose, raccoon, skunk, woodchuck,* and *teepee*.

From the French we obtained such words as *gopher, caribou,* and *pumpkin*. Because the French were great travelers and explorers they left our language with many words related to their travels: *portage, voyageur, prairie, levee, coulee, butte, bayou,* and *toboggan*.

The Spanish gave us *alfalfa, marijuana, bronco, burro, mustang, coyote, corral, lariat, lasso, ranch, poncho, chile con carne,* and *taco* (and a place to eat them called a *cafeteria*). They also left us a few words related to jails and the legal system: *calaboose, desperado, hoosegow, incommunicado,* and *vigilantes*.

Many Dutch people settled in the Hudson River Valley in New York State beginning in the middle 1600s. From these early Dutch settlers our language gained *cole slaw, cookie, waffle, sleigh, caboose,* and *stoop* (porch). The Dutch also gave us the word *Yankee*, which comes from the Dutch *Jan kees—John Cheese*—a term applied to the New Englanders at times by the Dutch.

Beginning as early as 1683, thousands of German immigrants flooded into this country, bringing with them such words as *delicatessen, frankfurter, hamburger, liverwurst, noodle, pretzel,* and *sauerkraut*. Lest you believe all the Germans did was eat, they also gave us the educationally related words *semester* and *seminar*. The prefix *ker-* and the suffix *-fest* also are traced to the Germans and had considerable influence on at least our informal language: *kerflop, kerplunk, kersmash* and *gabfest, talkfest,* and *slugfest*. With the African slaves came thousands of words, including *gumbo, goober, voodoo,* and *hoodoo*.

The Scandinavians gave us *smorgasbord* and *lutefisk,* the Italians *ravioli* and *minestrone*.[5] And we could go on.

The point of this is to make word study interesting. It is not a task that is always dull and uninteresting. Because words in our language are symbols, that is, represent something, we can discover not only the meaning but also something about the history of the words—their origins. This historical digging can give life and interest to a task that otherwise might be thought of as exceedingly boring and uninteresting.

HOW WORDS ARE LEARNED

Before we outline some ideas on how to increase your vocabulary, we must in all honesty say that there is no simple, painless way to acquire and master a good vocabulary. Though the process can be made interesting, as we've pointed out above, it is nevertheless time-consuming and hard. There are no real shortcuts to the process, either, although as we'll point out later, there are some techniques that can make the process less arduous.

All of us have at least four vocabularies: the words we speak; the words we write; the words we read and recognize; and the words we read, recognize, but whose meanings we are not sure of. The words that remain are obviously those that we've not seen before and don't know.

Walter Pauk suggests that one process of learning new words is to concentrate on what he calls the "frontier words." Pauk says that the degree of difficulty in learning new words does not depend on the number of syllables they have, how they are pronounced, or their geographic origin. He believes the degree of difficulty in learning new words depends on the complexity of the ideas they represent. What this implies, then, is that not only do we learn new words by providing simple synonyms, but also we must learn the ideas the words represent.[6]

A PROCESS FOR WORD SLEUTHING

The means of word sleuthing, of discovering the meaning of new words—and providing the impetus for using them—depend on a dictionary frame of mind. That is, you must be comfortable with and become old friends with a good dictionary. Several dictionaries are available that could be recommended. At least one of these should have a prominent place on your study desk:

The American College Dictionary, Random House
Webster's New Collegiate Dictionary, Merriam
The American Heritage Dictionary of the English Language, American Heritage and Houghton Mifflin

Besides having one of these desk dictionaries handy, you should also never hesitate to use one of the larger, unabridged dictionaries located in public and college libraries. Good one-volume unabridged dictionaries include:

Webster's New International Dictionary of the English Language, Merriam
New Standard Dictionary of the English Language, Funk and Wagnalls

As mentioned earlier, if you want to trace the historical beginnings of a word in depth, the *Oxford English Dictionary* (Clarendon Press, Oxford, England) is likely the most outstanding source.

Learning Words from Their Contexts

Three approaches may be followed for determining the meaning of a word in the context in which it is written: (1) definition, (2) inference, and (3) contrast.

Definition Often, when an author introduces a new word, particularly if it is a technical word, the author will define the word when it is used. If the word is not defined directly, there is often sufficient explanation of the word so that you can determine its meaning. To check your ability to determine the meanings of words from author's direct or indirect definitions, complete the following exercise.

WORD CONTEXT QUIZ (DETECTING AUTHORS' DEFINITIONS)*

Directions: In your own words, write the meaning of the underscored words in the following sentences. Also indicate the clues.

1 The majority of organisms are aerobic; that is, they require oxygen to release the energy for life functions.

_____

_____

2 After age forty some men increase their amount of bed rest to the point where it actually becomes enervating. The man who gets more than eight or nine hours of sleep will probably have less energy than the man who gets fewer hours of sleep.

_____

_____

WORD CONTEXT QUIZ (DETECTING AUTHORS' DEFINITIONS)* (*Cont.*)

3 The characters created and developed by a writer need not be based on actual people, but they must have <u>verisimilitude</u>, or plausibility.

_____

_____

4 The great religions all share the common purpose of producing a <u>metanoia</u>, a change of spirit.

_____

_____

* Adapted from Nancy B. Davis, *Basic Vocabulary Skills*, McGraw-Hill, New York, 1969, pp. 125 and 127. Used with permission of McGraw-Hill Book Company.

Example 1 Without going to the dictionary to look up *aerobic*, we can figure out from the sentence that aerobic means *requiring oxygen*. The clue in the sentence is the phrase "that is."

Example 2 This example is not quite as easy. The author does not define the word *enervating*. The second sentence of the example deals with energy and its relationship to the amount of sleep a man receives. We could deduce from this clue that *enervating* likely means *causing to lose energy*. But we'd want to check the dictionary to make sure.

Example 3 The clue to defining *verisimilitude* is the word *or*. *Verisimilitude* means *plausibility* or *the appearance of truth*.

Example 4 *Metanoia* is defined for us too. The comma after the underlined word is our clue. *Metanoia* means *change of spirit*.

Inference We really become word sleuths when the clues to the word meanings are not as obvious as those mentioned above but are nevertheless present. Complete the following quiz to check our ability to deal with the more subtle clues to word definitions.

WORD CONTEXT QUIZ (DETECTING INFERENCES)*

Directions: In your own words, write the meaning of the underscored words in the following sentences. Also indicate the clues.

1 A person may hold a certain philosophy but not be able to <u>articulate</u> it, at least not always in words.

_____

_____

2 It is likely that both <u>olfactory</u> and taste sensitivity are involved in food selec-

WORD CONTEXT QUIZ (DETECTING INFERENCES)* (*Cont.*)

tion. The problem of taking that first bite of limburger cheese serves as an example.

_____

3 In his lectures Sullivan typically <u>eschewed</u> the obvious in favor of the obscure.

_____

4 Important <u>pedagogical</u> purposes can be served by the essay-type examination because students learn to organize their ideas and improve their style of expression.

_____

_____

* Adapted from Nancy B. Davis, *Basic Vocabulary Skills*, McGraw-Hill, New York, 1969, p. 126. Used with permission of McGraw-Hill Book Company.

How did you do? Were you able to figure out the definitions of the underlined words from the contextual clues?

Example 1   You might guess that *articulate* has something to do with words. It means *to speak clearly*. The clue is "not able . . . in words."

Example 2   The strong clue in the sentence is "Limburger cheese," which to most people triggers the sense of smell. *Olfactory* means *sense of smell*.

Example 3   *Eschewed* may have been a bit more difficult. It means *passed over* or *shunned*. The clue in the sentence is "in favor of."

Example 4   "Students learn" is the clue in this example. *Pedagogical* means *teaching* or *educational*.

Contrast   The third way of determining the meanings of words from their context is to look for contrast, that is, to look for a word in the sentence that contrasts with the word you don't know. Of course this assumes that you know one of the contrasting words.

WORD CONTEXT QUIZ (DETECTING CONTRAST)*

Directions: In your own words, write the meaning of the underscored words in the following sentences. Also indicate the clues.
1 Meditation is generally favored by the Roman Catholic, but in general the Protestant will <u>abjure</u> it.

_____

_____

WORD CONTEXT QUIZ (DETECTING CONTRAST)* (*Cont.*)

2 The term sea usually implies that waters are <u>saline</u>, but the Sea of Galilee is not salty.

_____

_____

3 We can now summarize our discussion by this statement: that which is used develops, and that which is not used <u>atrophies</u>.

_____

_____

4 The pictorial aspect of art may be important, but it is not the significant factor which separates <u>mundane</u> art from great art.

_____

_____

* Adapted from Nancy B. Davis, *Basic Vocabulary Skills*, McGraw-Hill, New York, 1969, pp. 126, 128, 129. Used with permission of McGraw-Hill Book Company.

Example 1   The clue words in this sentence are "favored . . . but." *Abjure* means *reject* or *avoid*.

Example 2   *Saline* means *salty*. The clues are "but . . . not salty."

Example 3   *Atrophies* means *wastes away* or *deteriorates*. Clues are "which is used . . . which is not used."

Example 4   *Mundane* means *ordinary*. Clues are "which separates . . . from."

With some practice you should be able to figure out the meanings of many words from their context if you apply the three principles of definition, inference, and contrast.

Another approach to word sleuthing that many people find useful is determining the meaning of words from their prefixes and roots.

Learning Words from Prefixes and Roots

It is estimated that some 60 percent of the English language is made up partly or totally of prefixes and roots derived from Latin and Greek. It would follow, then, that some working understanding of the most common prefixes and roots would be helpful in word sleuthing.

For example, if you know that the root word *graph* means *to write,* you can derive the beginnings of a definition for the following words:

biography: written account of a person's life
cartography: mapmaking (writing with map symbols)
graphology: study of handwriting
graphospasm: writers' cramp

monograph: written account of a single thing
phonograph: writing with sound
photography: picture writing
stenographer: writer of shorthand
telegraph: writing at a distance

And likewise, if you know that the prefix *retro* means *back* or *backward,* you can begin to define the following words:

retroflex: turned backward
retrograde: to turn back
retrogress: to move backward
retrolental: behind a lens
retropack: spacecraft rockets designed to reduce craft's speed
retrorse: bent downward or backward
retrospect: a review of past events
retroversion: turned backward

The practical advantage of knowing prefixes and roots is being able to use a few basic definitions that are found again and again in the English language. When you find a word that is entirely foreign to you and you go to the dictionary to find its meaning, do not overlook the information that is offered concerning the prefixes and roots of that word. This information may be invaluable in helping you discover the meanings of other new words that have the same root and/or prefix.

Tables 6-1 through 6-3 give examples of common prefixes, roots, and number sources that you will find repeated in your reading.

TABLE 6-1
PREFIXES FROM GREEK AND LATIN

Prefix	Meaning	Example	Definition
a	not	asexual	lacking sex
ab	from, away	abnormal	deviating from normal
ad	to, toward	adsorb	take up
ambi	both, around, about	ambient	encompassing
ante	before	antebellum	before a war
anti	against	antianxiety	preventing anxiety
bene	well, good	beneficient	doing good
bi	two, twice	bicentric	having two centers
cata	down, downward	catacomb	underground passageway
circum	around, about	circumfuse	pour around
com	with or together	combo	combination

TABLE 6-1

PREFIXES FROM GREEK AND LATIN—CONTINUED

Prefix	Meaning	Example	Definition
contra	against, opposite	contraband	illegal or prohibited
de	down, from	deflect	bend down or aside
dia	through	diagnose	determine nature or cause
dis	apart from, separation	disembark	put ashore
em	in, inside	embrace	hug
epi	upon, above	epidermis	outer layer of skin
eu	well, good	eulogize	write in high praise
ex	out	excerpt	take extracts from
extra	outside, beyond	extraneous	from the outside
hemi	half	hemisphere	half of the earth
hyper	above, excessive	hyperbole	exaggeration
hypo	under, less	hypogeal	growing underground
in	in, on	inboard	toward the inside
in	not	incommodious	not convenient
inter	between	interact	act upon one another
mal	bad	malfunction	function imperfectly
mis	wrong	mislabel	label incorrectly
mono	one, alone	monorail	one rail
multi	many, much	multicolored	having various colors
non	not	nonsense	no meaning (sense)
ob	against, facing	obverse	facing the observer
out	external, beyond	outmoded	not in style
over	over, above	overcast	having a covering of clouds
pan	all, every	panhuman	pertaining to all humanity
para	beside, resembling	parable	story illustrating moral principle
post	after, behind	postdoctoral	beyond doctoral level
per	through, thoroughly	perforate	make a hole through
poly	many	polyandric	having many husbands
pre	before	preschool	nursery school
pro	for, forth, in favor	profuse	pouring forth
pseudo	false	pseudonym	fictitious name
re	back, again	reenact	perform again
retro	back, backward	retrogress	move backward
se	apart, away	secure	safe from danger
semi	half, partly	semierect	incompletely upright
sub	under, below	submerge	put under water
super	over, above	supervisor	one who oversees
syn	with, together	synergy	combined action
trans	across, beyond	transmit	send or transfer
ultra	beyond, excessively	ultrapure	having utmost purity
un	not, reversal	unaffected	not influenced
under	below, beneath	underpinning	basis, support
vice	instead of	vice regent	regent's deputy

Source: Adapted from Nancy B. Davis, *Basic Vocabulary Skills*, McGraw-Hill, New York, 1969, pp. 92–94. Used with permission of McGraw-Hill Book Company.

TABLE 6-2
ROOTS FROM GREEK AND LATIN

Root	Meaning	Example	Definition
act	do or drive	interact	act upon another
amb	walk	perambulator	one who travels on foot
annu	year	semiannual	twice yearly
anthrop	human being	misanthrope	one who dislikes people
aqu	water	aquifer	water-bearing rock
aud	hear	audition	a critical listening
auto	self	automatic	self-acting
bibl	book	bibliopole	dealer in rare books
capt, capit	head	decapitate	cut off the head
cent	a hundred	centennial	100th anniversary
chrom	color	monochrome	of one color
cid	cut or kill	homicide	killing of one human by another
civi	citizen	uncivil	not civilized, rude
cracy, crat	strength	democracy	power vested in the people
cycl	circle, wheel	bicycle	two-wheeled vehicle
duc, duct	lead	educate	teach
equ	equal, even	equitable	dealing fairly and equally
fac	do or make	facile	easily accomplished
fer	carry or bear	transfer	convey
graph	write	typography	something produced by letterpress
hem	blood	hemophilia	hereditary blood defect
junct	join	conjuncture	union
liber	free	liberate	set free
med	middle	medial	in the middle
mit	send	transmit	send or transfer
mo	move	demote	move downward
nov	new	innovation	something new
omni	all	omnificent	all powerful
plic	fold	explicate	unfold
rupt	break	disrupt	break apart
tele	distant	telephoto	photography at a distance
ten	hold or keep	retention	act of keeping
tend, tens	stretch	tense	stretched tight
tors, tort	twist or wind	contort	twist in violent manner
tract	draw or pull	retract	draw back
val	strength, worth	convalesce	grow strong
ven, vent	come	eventuate	come out finally
vert, vers	turn or change	convert	transform, turn around
vid, vis	see	envisage	view in certain way
vital	life	devitalize	deprive of life
voc	call or summon	vociferate	call out loudly
volv, volut	roll	evolution	process of change

Source: Adapted from Nancy B. Davis, *Basic Vocabulary Skills,* McGraw-Hill, New York, 1969, pp. 94–99. Used with permission of McGraw-Hill Book Company.

TABLE 6-3
GREEK AND LATIN NUMBER SOURCES

Number	Latin	Examples	Greek	Examples
1	uni	uniformity, university	mon, mono	monocular, monograph
2	du	duplex, duplicity	di	dichotomy, dilemma
3	tri	trident, trinity	same as Latin	same as Latin
4	quad, quat	quadrivium, quaternity	tetra	tetraploid, tetratheism
5	quin	quinquennial, quintessence	penta	pentagon, pentaploid
6	sex	sexennial, sextuplicate	hex	hexagon, hexapod
7	sept	September, septennial	hept	heptameter
8	oct	octal, October	same as Latin	same as Latin
9	nov	November, novena	enne	ennead
10	dec	decade	same as Latin	same as Latin

Source: Adapted from Nancy B. Davis, *Basic Vocabulary Skills,* McGraw-Hill, New York, 1969, pp. 99–100. Used with permission of McGraw-Hill Book Company.

A TECHNIQUE FOR LEARNING NEW WORDS

A simple technique for learning the new words you will meet in your reading, when you go to lectures, and when you talk to people is suggested by Pauk.[7]

The system involves the use of 3- by 5-inch note cards.

1 When you meet a new word, write on a 3- by 5-inch card the word and the sentence in which it is found. Underline the new word.

2 Put only one new word on a card, and when you have several of these words go to the dictionary.

3 On the side of the card where you have written the word and the sentence in which it is found, copy from the dictionary the word with its syllables and diacritical markings indicated. They will help you learn how to pronounce the word. Do not put anything further on this side of the card.

4 On the reverse side of the card, indicate the prefix and root definitions if they are available for the word.

5 Write the definitions of the word that the dictionary indicates, and check the definition that fits the word as it is used in your original sentence.

6 Carry several of these cards with you. When you are waiting for the bus, waiting for a lecture to begin, walking between classes, etc., refer to the cards.

7 Try to define the word in your own words, then look at the other side of the card to check your accuracy.

8 You might consider keeping a file of these cards that can be reviewed from time to time.

9 Attempt to use the word, first in your writing and then in your speaking. It is through use that the new word will eventually become a part of your vocabulary and will become an old friend like the rest of the words in your working vocabulary.

SUMMARY

In this chapter we have discussed words, tools the returning student will use constantly.

Words may be classified according to their degree of formality—vulgate, informal, or formal—and according to how they are used—in speaking, writing, or thinking.

Approaches often used to learn new words include vocabulary books, reading, natural growth, word lists, dictionary study, and becoming a word sleuth. Digging into the history of words often adds interest to vocabulary building.

Becoming a word sleuth involves developing a dictionary frame of mind. One can determine the meaning of new words from the context in which they are written by looking for definitions, inferences, and contrasts. One may also learn new words by becoming acquainted with common prefixes and roots. The use of note cards to record new words met while reading can be a useful aid to building vocabulary.

REFERENCES

1 Porter G. Perrin, *Writer's Guide and Index to English*, Scott, Foresman, Chicago, 1950.

2 David Wallechinsky and Irving Wallace, *The People's Almanac*, Doubleday, New York.

3 *Oxford English Dictionary*, Clarendon Press, Oxford, England, complete edition, 1933.

4 Webb Garrison, *What's in a Word*, Abingdon, New York, 1965, pp. 272 and 274.

5 Albert H. Marckwardt, *American English*, Oxford University Press, New York, 1958.

6 Walter Pauk, *How to Study in College*, Houghton Mifflin, Boston, 1974.

7 Ibid., pp. 96–99.

CHAPTER 7

USING RESOURCES EFFECTIVELY

Learning what resources are available and how to use them is a skill that will help you immeasurably no matter what area of study you pursue. But some returning students are reluctant to ask about resources that are available to them.

Some of this reluctance is based on the attitude that 40-year-old persons should not ask questions and seek help, but should know how to do things on their own. If you are someone who has this attitude, toss it away. If it would help, think of the resources as something you've helped pay for, probably through taxes, and surely through the tuition money you've paid the institution. These resources are as much yours as any other student's. As difficult as this may be to accept, it is entirely proper for a 40-year-old student to ask questions about resources and to go to those resources with questions. Using resources is part of being a student. Everyone, whether or not a formal student, uses resources constantly. When we look for an address we check a phone book. When we travel we use a map. When we want help with our income tax we ask a tax consultant. So it is entirely proper, in fact expected, that you will know what resources are available at your school and you will know how to use them.

A place to begin to learn about your school's resources is to ask if a "resource directory" is available. At the University of Wisconsin-Madison, students are given copies of *The Wheat and the Chaff: A Campus Source Book* when they enroll. This book, which is revised each year, lists resources available on the campus in the following areas: academics, counseling, employment, finances, foreign students, government, health, housing, information resources, minorities, protection, social life, transportation, and campus rules. The resources are listed with a description of how to use them and what assistance you can expect from each.

In this chapter examples of many resources you can expect to find at most schools are listed. Attention is given to those resources that will be of most help to you with your academic work.

STUDENT RESOURCES

Sometimes the most overlooked resource at any school is the students themselves. And the most overlooked resource of all is *you* and the experiences you've had so far during your life.

You and Your Experiences

You and your experiences are one of the most valuable resources you have. Often you'll meet a question in your reading or during a class that you've dealt with sometime during your life. Perhaps you ran into something similar during a work experience you had or during a trip you took to Europe, for example.

Unfortunately some students have the mistaken notion that the experiences they've had don't count or aren't potential resources for answers to questions they face in their academic studies. One of the advantages of being an older student is the wealth of experiences you've had during your life. Putting the new information you are gaining into the framework of these experiences and using these experiences to help you understand new information, concepts, and theories can help to make learning challenging, exciting, and more real to you.

Other Students

You will quickly learn to know a fairly large number of students through your contacts with them in class and discussion groups; some will be older and others much younger than you. But all of them are potential resources for you if you allow them to be.

You can meet with a small group of students after a lecture, perhaps over coffee, to discuss the lecture you have just heard and to compare notes.

You can join an organized group of students, such as a single-parent student group or a graduate-student group.

You can consult with students who have taken a course that you are planning to take to find out directly what is in the course, how they liked the course, something about the professor and the way he or she teaches, the types of examinations given, and so on. This "inside information" is invaluable in planning what courses to take.

You can meet with a group of students to help prepare for examinations. Of course you will have to prepare on your own as well. But other students can help by acting as "sounding boards" and seeing if you understand concepts as they do. Some students may have had considerably more experience in certain content areas than you have had, and they can help you by providing additional background information.

One word of caution: It is easy for student groups to degenerate into "bitch sessions" or "bull sessions." To make student group work most effective, the students in the group should plan an agenda for their activities. They should decide what questions or issues they will discuss and police each other to make sure they stay on the topic. They should also assign to each other tasks that the members then bring back to the group for discussion.

Unfortunately, in some academic settings, students develop a competitive attitude toward each other rather than one that is cooperative. Sometimes a few students have to take the initiative in organizing a student group, to help move past the attitude of competition. So much can be gained by students working together on common problems and questions that it is depressing when students believe that helping another student will somehow lessen their ability to attain a good grade.

STAFF RESOURCES

The academic staff is usually more than happy to assist students with problems and questions. Some students overlook this rather obvious resource or believe that the staff either is too busy or isn't available to assist them. True, an occasional professor may not have time to work with you at the time that you choose. But usually, if you can plan ahead a little, nearly all professors will help you.

Major Professor

In most academic departments, each student is assigned to a major professor or adviser. This staff person has the responsibility for helping you plan your study schedule: what courses to take, the sequence of courses, the requirements for graduation, and so on. This person is also almost always available to help you with any academic problem you may have. Of course your major professor doesn't always have the answer you seek, but he or she usually knows a resource that you can consult. Learn your major professor's office hours, and make an appointment when you wish to have a conference.

Course Instructors

Questions about material you don't understand in a course should be raised with the course instructor. Sometimes this is not possible to do during the regular class period. If that is the case, talk with the instructor after class or make an appointment to talk with him or her later. Most instructors welcome the opportunity to talk with students about questions that grow out of their classes, yet many students are reluctant to talk with them out of class.

Of course common sense must be followed too. If the answer to your question can be gotten by consulting your textbook or talking with another student, obviously do this first. But don't be reluctant to consult your instructor if the question remains unanswered.

Other Professors

Professors who are not your course instructors are available to you if you seek them out. If you are working on a paper and you know that an authority in the content area you are researching is on your campus, by all means make an appointment and discuss the questions you have. This person may have the freshest, most up-to-date information that is available on the topic.

And don't be reluctant to contact professors at other colleges and universities whom you know have information you need. Write to them, make an appointment and go visit them if this is possible, or even call them on the phone and raise your questions with them.

As is true with all resource people, the more specific you can be with your questions, the more help you are likely to receive.

HELPING CENTERS

Most colleges and universities have various helping centers designed to assist students with problems. Some of these centers are multipurpose; that is, they deal with such topics as career planning and personal problems as well as academic problems facing students. Others are more specific, focusing specifically on such problems as writing or study skills. Below are listed five types of helping centers. On some campuses the functions performed by these centers are combined into one.

Study Skills Centers

These centers deal with such topics as how to take lecture notes, how to read a textbook, how to plan a study schedule, how to prepare for and take an exam, and how to write academic papers—many of the same topics covered in this book.

Instructors are available to work with students individually or in groups. In some schools, study skills classes are available for students to review study skills and improve those in which they feel somewhat deficient.

Today, taking part in study skills programs such as those suggested above is routintely done by many students, not only those who are having difficulty. Students with average or even above average study skills can increase their skills considerably by enrolling in programs such as these. They are not designed only for the student who is experiencing difficulty.

Writing Laboratories

If you have problems with the basics of acceptable writing—sentence structure, grammar, punctuation—or with organization, with how to do the research for a paper, or with how to properly document research reports, then a writing laboratory may be of assistance. These laboratories are common on most campuses and are designed to assist students no matter what their writing problem may be. Most are organized informally, with an instructor working with you on an individual basis. Often the actual papers you are writing for your courses are used as examples in these laboratories.

See Chapter 4 in this book for information that will assist you in improving your writing competency.

Reading Clinics

Most campuses have reading clinics for those students who wish to increase the speed at which they read as well as improve their comprehension level. These clinics often emphasize the different skills required for reading different kinds of material: research reports, literature, essays, and popular material.

See Chapter 3 for detailed information on how to improve your reading skills.

Counseling Centers

Every campus has a counseling center designed to help students with whatever problem they may be facing. Often the counseling center can be a good place to start with a problem, no matter what its nature. The counselors at the center are well informed about the helping resources that are available on your campus and in your community and will help you to find the right one to assist you with your problem.

Returning-Student Center

In recent years many colleges and universities have opened special offices for the returning student. These centers, often staffed by counselors who are themselves returning adults, are available to assist with career planning, admission to a college, registration procedures, financial aid, and child care information. They also sponsor study skills workshops, value clarification sessions, and testing programs designed to assist in career planning and evaluation.

In addition to these functions, they serve as a referral office for any problem you may have that they cannot solve.

LIBRARIES

Without question one of the most important resources for any student is the library. Every student knows this, yet many have problems in understanding what resources they can expect a library to have and how they go about obtaining these resources without spending hours doing it.

What to Expect

Following is a list of what you can generally expect to find in a college or university library. In many instances, not all of these resources will be found in the same building but will be distributed among several library buildings on the campus.

1 A collection of books relating to the subject-matter areas that are taught at the college or university. (Many of these are kept on reserve shelves for specific courses.)

2 A collection of general books, not relating specifically to a given subject-matter area.

3 Reference books of a general nature and those related specifically to subject-matter areas emphasized at the college or university.

4 Periodicals and newspapers, including current issues and bound volumes. In some libraries, older issues are on microfilm and Microcards.

5 Pamphlets and clippings.

6 Government publications.

7 Audiovisual materials: films, slides, filmstrips, records, tapes, maps, and globes.

8 Microforms, such as microfilm, Microcards, and microfiche.

9 Archival materials related to the institution.

10 Books for recreational reading.

Types of Libraries

On most campuses you can expect to find more than one library. On some of the larger campuses you will find several, some quite general and others quite highly specialized.

There is usually one general library that services the entire college or university. In this library are located the major reference works, general collections of books, government publications, periodicals, and newspapers. If this is the only library on campus, then the other resources listed above will be located there as well.

In addition to the general library, larger campuses also have college or school libraries, such as a law library, an engineering library, a medical library, or an agriculture library.

Many college departments also have departmental libraries, in which collections are maintained which pertain specifically to the subject matter of that department; examples are a dairy science library and an art history library.

As an example, here are the major libraries at the University of Wisconsin-Madison. This list doesn't include the many departmental libraries.

1 Memorial Library   A general library serving the entire campus. It includes general book collections, a large reference center, periodical and newspaper collection, and microfiches.

2 College Library   A library designed primarily for undergraduate students. It includes a large reserve book section for students with required reading associated with courses they are taking. It also includes collections related to feminist concerns—paperbacks, magazines, and newsletters—and an ethnic collection with particular emphasis on materials related to native Americans, black Americans, Spanish-speaking Americans, and Asian Americans. There is a tape center where students, through a remote-access system, can listen individually to music and readings from literature.

   3 Agriculture Library
   4 Art Library
   5 Biology Library
   6 Business Library
   7 Chemistry Library
   8 Clinical Sciences Center Library
   9 Engineering Library
  10 Geography Library
  11 Geology Library
  12 Historical Library
  13 Law Library

14 Library School Library
15 Math Library
16 Medical Library
17 Music Library
18 Observatory Library
19 Pharmacy Library
20 Physics Library
21 Social Work Library

In addition to these libraries, students also have access to the State Historical Society Library, located on campus, and to the Madison Public Library, which has a collection of 250,000 books.

Some campuses will have more libraries than the University of Wisconsin-Madison. Others will have less. But one of your first tasks as a returning student is to find out what libraries are available on your campus, where they are located, what resources they have, and how you can obtain the resources.

Layout of a Library

Once you've learned what libraries are available at your college or university and which ones are most likely to be ones you will be using, you should plan a tour to get acquainted with each one. In most libraries, you will find the following areas:

1 *Catalog Room*   This is the heart of the library, for here are listed all the materials in the library, with the exception of some periodicals, and the locations where you can find them.

2 *Reference Works*   If not a special room or rooms, there is a special area set aside for reference works such as dictionaries, encyclopedias, indexes, yearbooks, and directories. These materials usually are not permitted to circulate, so working areas are associated with the reference collection.

3 *Study or Reading Rooms*   Many students find these the most conducive areas for study of all the many places where students may study on campus. Also, in some libraries, it is possible to rent study carrels, where a student may keep study materials and use them on a regular basis. Often, though, these study carrels are reserved for advanced graduate students and faculty members.

4 *Periodical Rooms*   Here are stored current issues of magazines, journals, and newspapers and bound collections of past issues.

5 *The Stacks*   The areas where the major collection of books and usually the bound periodicals are kept. You need to find out if the stacks are open or closed. The term *open stacks* means that you can enter the shelves

area of the library and find books by yourself. With *closed stacks* you may not enter the shelves area, but assistants will find the books for you. Many libraries are moving to an open-stacks policy, so it becomes important for you to know how the collection is stored. Libraries have available maps that not only show the location of all the various areas in the library but also show you which categories of books are stored where.

6 *Audiovisual Materials*   Tapes, slides, films, and microforms are often stored in a separate area of the library, with the necessary equipment for seeing or listening nearby.

Card Catalog

If you are looking for a book in a library, the first place to begin is the card catalog. It will not only help you find a specific book that you are looking for, but it will also help you find books in a given subject-matter area where you don't know the authors or titles.

Generally, you can expect to find three types of cards in card catalogs: author cards, title cards, and subject cards. Most publications have at least two entries in the card catalog: an entry under the author's name and an entry under the title *or* subject.

Author Card   The author card is the main entry for any publication. In general, you can expect to find the following information on the author card:

1 The call number, which indicates where the book may be found in the library.

2 Author's full name, inverted, the date of birth, and the date of death if the author is not living. The author may be (a) an individual, (b) an individual who edits rather than writes the work, (c) an institution or an organization (such as U.S. Department of Agriculture or Green Valley Community College), (d) a committee (such as the Committee on Adult Learning), (e) a title of a publication (such as *National Geographic Magazine*).

3 The title and the subtitle of the book.

4 The coauthor, illustrator, or translator.

5 The imprint, which includes the place of publication, the publisher, and the date of publication.

6 The collation, which includes the number of pages or volumes, the illustrative materials, and the size of the book in centimeters.

7 The series to which the book belongs, if it is one of a series.

8 The subjects that are treated fully in the book.

9 The full name and birth and death dates of the coauthor, translator, editor, and illustrator.[1]

This information is printed or typed on 3- by 5-inch cards and filed alphabetically in trays according to the last name of the author. (See Figure 7-1.)

Title Card   The title card is prepared for a book that has a distinctive title. The title of the book is typed above the author's name on the title card.

Subject Card   The number of subject cards for a particular book depends on the number of subjects that are discussed fully in the book. Generally, a subject card is made for each subject that is discussed fully. Usually, the subject is typed at the top of the card in red capital and small letters or in black capital letters. The remainder of the card is the same as the author card.[2]

Most persons know how to find a book when they know the author and title; fewer know how to go to the subject catalog to find specific authors and titles under subject-matter areas they are researching. If you are

Figure 7-1
Author card. (Jean Key Gates, *Guide to the Use of Books and Libraries*, McGraw-Hill Book Company, New York, 1974, p. 63. Used with permission of McGraw-Hill Book Company.)

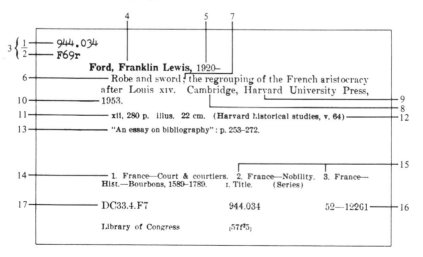

Figure 1 Author card or main entry: (1) class number; (2) author or book number and title letter; (3) call number; (4) author's name, inverted; (5) author's date of birth; (6) title of book; (7) subtitle; (8) place of publication; (9) publisher; (10) date of publication; (11) collation; (12) series note; (13) bibliographical note; (14) subject heading (the subject treated fully); (15) other subjects treated; (16) Library of Congress catalog card number; (17) Library of Congress classification and author number.

writing a paper on a topic and don't know any authors or titles within that subject area, the subject catalog is one place to start.

Also, if you find a listing of one book that deals with the topic of interest and go to the stacks searching for that book (assuming an open-stack policy at your library), you will usually find many more books on that topic stored on the same shelf. A few minutes spent browsing the shelves can be very profitable.

Classification Systems

Library materials are generally stored according to the Dewey Decimal classification or the Library of Congress classification.

In the Dewey Decimal classification, numbers are used to divide documents into general categories and then into more specific categories.

Dewey Decimal Classification

000–099	General works: bibliographies, encyclopedias, periodicals
100–199	Philosophy: metaphysics, psychology, logic, ethics
200–299	Religion: Bible, theology, Christian churches
300–399	Social science: political science, economics, education
400–499	Philology: comparative philology, English language, various languages
500–599	Pure science: mathematics, physics, chemistry, biology
600–699	Applied science: medicine, engineering, agriculture
700–799	Arts and recreation: architecture, sculpture, painting
800–899	Literature: American literature, English literature, other literatures
900–999	History: geography, biography, ancient history, modern history[3]

The Library of Congress classification uses letters of the alphabet for broad categories and numbers for finer divisions. Within each subject category, a letter is used for the author's name and a serial number is used when there are several of the same initials within a category.

Library of Congress Classification

A	General works. AC, collections; AE, encyclopedias; AY, yearbooks; AZ, general history.
B	Philosophy-religion. BC, logic; BF, psychology; BL, religions.
C	History-auxiliary sciences. CB, civilization; CS, geneology; CT, biography.
D	History and topography. DA, Great Britain; DC, France; DK, Russia; DU, Australia and Oceania.
E–F	America. E, America (general) and United States (general); F, United States (local) and America except the United States.

G   Geography. GC, oceanography; GN, anthropology; GT, manners and customs; GV, sports and amusements.

H   Social sciences. HB, economic theory; HD, economic history; HE, transportation; HF, commerce; HG, finance; HM, sociology; HQ, family, marriage, home; HT, communities; HV, social pathology, philanthropy.

J   Political science. JA, general works; JO, theory of the state; JX, international law.

K   Law.

L   Education. LB, theory and practice; LC, special forms; LD, United States.

M   Music. ML, literature of music; MT, musical instruction.

N   Fine Arts. NA, architecture; NC, painting; NK, industrial arts.

P   Language and literature. PA, classical languages; PC, romance languages; PD, Teutonic languages; PR, English literature; PS, American literature.

Q   Science. QA, mathematics; QC, physics; QD, chemistry; QE, geology; QL, zoology; QP, physiology.

R   Medicine. RB, pathology; RE, ophthalmology; RK, dentistry; RM, therapeutics; RT, nursing.

S   Agriculture—plant and animal industry. SB, plant culture; SD, forestry; SF, animal culture; SK, hunting sports.

T   Technology. TA, engineering; TH, building construction; TK, electrical engineering; TN, mineral industries; TR, photography.

U   Military science.

V   Naval science.

Z   Bibliography and Library Science.[4]

Reference Books

The library's reference books are resources you will use again and again. Although most libraries have reference librarians to assist you in finding materials, the sooner you develop the skill to use these materials independently the more efficiently you will be able to pursue answers to your questions.

Reference books can be divided into two broad categories, those that are general in scope and not limited to a specific subject and those that are specific to a given subject area, such as history, art, science, or literature. No attempt is made to indicate the many references available in specific subject-matter fields. The books below are valuable in providing lists of references classified according to various subject fields:

Cook, Margaret G; *The New Library Key,* H. W. Wilson, New York, 1975.

Gates, Jean Key: *Guide to the Use of Books and Libraries,* 4th ed., McGraw-Hill, New York, 1979.

McCormick, Mona: *Who-What-When-Where-How-Why-Made Easy,* Quadrangle, New York, 1971.

Sheehy, Eugene P., *Guide to Reference Books,* American Library Association, Chicago, 1976.

Below is a list of the types of general reference books you can expect to find in a college library and a brief description of the purposes they serve.

Dictionaries   Dictionaries provide information about words: meanings, spelling, pronunciation, usage, syllabification, and derivation. They may be unabridged, such as *Webster's Third New International Dictionary,* Merriam, Springfield, Mass., 1971, and *Funk & Wagnalls New Standard Dictionary of the English Language,* Funk & Wagnalls, New York, 1963; or they may be smaller, desk-type dictionaries that are less complete than the unabridged editions.

Encyclopedias   Encyclopedias are concerned with subjects and provide an overview of a topic that includes definition, background, description, and bibliographic references. Examples:

The Encyclopedia Americana, Americana Corporation, New York, 1973. 30 vols.

Encyclopedia Britannica, Encyclopedia Britannica, Chicago, 1973. 24 vols.

Indexes   Indexes provide guides to where information can be found. They are particularly useful in finding articles that appear in periodicals. Examples:

Readers' Guide to Periodical Literature, H. W. Wilson, New York, 1900–.

Book Review Digest, H. W. Wilson, New York, 1905–.

Yearbooks   Yearbooks, sometimes called *annuals,* present information about the events of the past year. Examples:

Collier's Year Book, Collier, New York, 1938–.

U.S. Bureau of the Census: *Statistical Abstract of the United States,* U.S. Government Printing Office, Washington, D.C., 1878–.

Handbooks   Handbooks are small books that provide a variety of information. Sometimes they are called *manuals* or *compendiums.* Examples:

Robert, Henry M.: *Robert's Rules of Order Newly Revised,* Scott, Foresman, Glenview, Ill., 1970.

United States Government Organization Manual, U.S. Government Printing Office, Washington, D.C., 1935–.

Almanacs   Almanacs were developed originally as a projection of the coming year day by day, with weather forecasts, moon phases, major holidays, and the like. Today almanacs include collections of miscellaneous facts and statistical information. Examples:

Information Please Almanac, Simon & Schuster, New York, 1947–.
The World Almanac and Book of Facts, Newspaper Enterprise Association, Inc., New York, 1868–.

Biographical Dictionaries   Biographical dictionaries are short excerpts about the lives of individuals, arranged alphabetically according to surnames. Examples:

The International Who's Who, 41 eds., Europa and Allen and Unwin, London, 1935–1977.
Who's Who in America, Marquis–Who's Who, Inc., Chicago, 1899–.

Directories   Directories list names and addresses of persons, organizations, agencies, institutions, and the like. They may also include purposes, names of officers, and contact persons. Examples:

Directory of American Scholars, 5th ed., Bowker, New York, 1969, 4 vols.
National Referral Center for Science and Technology: *A Directory of Information Resources in the United States,* U.S. Government Printing Office, Washington, D.C., 1964.

Atlases   An *atlas* is a bound collection of maps but also often includes pictures as well as tables and diagrams. Examples:

National Geographic Atlas of the World, rev. ed., National Geographic Society, Washington, D.C., 1970.
Rand McNally Cosmopolitan World Atlas, Rand McNally, Chicago, 1971.

Gazetteers   Gazetteers provide a list of place names, alphabetically arranged, with some information about each place. Information includes location and some historical or descriptive material. Examples:

Seltzer, L. E. (ed.): *The Columbia Lippincott Gazetteer of the World,* Columbia, New York, 1962.
Webster's New Geographical Dictionary, Merriam, Springfield, Mass., 1972.

Bibliographies   Bibliographies are lists of books and other materials on the same topic. They include author, title, publisher, number of pages, and often price. Sometimes bibliographies are annotated, that is, include a brief description of what each listing contains. Examples:

The Bibliographic Index, H. W. Wilson, New York, 1938–. Contains a listing of all current bibliographies, including those published in books, pamphlets, and periodical articles.[5]

Courtney, Winifred F. (ed.): *The Reader's Adviser,* 11th ed., Bowker, New York, 1969, 2 vols.

Library Aids

In addition to providing maps and general directions on how a particular library is organized and what rules prevail, many college libraries provide other aids.

The University of Wisconsin library provides guides designed to help the student use particular resources in the library or find materials on a given topic (see Figures 7-2 and 7-3).

MISCELLANEOUS RESOURCES

Students often overlook other resources that may be readily available to them.

College Bookstores

College bookstores not only serve as places where you can purchase textbooks, general books, and various types of supplies, but they also can provide you with an up-to-date source of information about new books available on a host of topics. Most college bookstores are organized according to such subject-matter areas as education, philosophy, psychology, history, and science. By browsing through the bookstore you may often get ideas about books you may later want to purchase or to check out of the library.

You can also learn about books that professors are recommending for courses you may take one day. By paging through the suggested textbooks, you can learn a considerable amount about the course itself.

Agencies, Institutions, and Businesses in the Community

If you are working on a paper for a course, you can often obtain practical information about the topic if you talk with someone who is working in the area. For example, if you are writing a paper on the professional education of engineers, you might talk with someone on your campus who is responsible for extension programs for engineers.

If you are working on a project related to social work, talking with a community social worker will give you practical insights and will likely

to find material on a subject

The Subject Catalog at Memorial is separate from the Author/Title Catalog and is located in the Langdon Street section of Room 224. To identify the correct subject term, use the red, two-volume <u>Library of Congress Subject Headings</u>, copies of which are located on the stands next to the Information Desk and near the Subject Catalog. This book lists the subject headings that might be used in the Memorial Library catalog. A term which is used as a subject heading is printed in dark ink. Terms which <u>cannot</u> be used are in light print, with the correct, accepted, term underneath, e.g.

> British literature
>   see English literature

Under the correct terms are frequently listed terms for related subjects which may be worth consulting. These headings are preceded by the symbols "s.a." (for more specific headings) and "xx" (for broader headings), e.g.

> Carpentry
>   s.a. Cabinet-work
>   Concrete construction
>   etc.
>   xx   Building
>   Joinery
>   etc.

A single "x" preceding a subject heading means that the term is not used, e.g.

> Adoption
>   x Child placing

Subject headings frequently have subdivisions, sometimes denoting the form of the material, e.g. English language - Dictionaries; sometimes indicating countries, historical periods or other aspects of the topic. A partial list of standard sub-headings is posted on the wall by the <u>Library of Congress Subject Headings</u>. These may be used with any subject where appropriate.

The subject headings assigned to a book are indicated by Arabic numerals at the bottom of the catalog card. These subject tracings may suggest other headings to check. Or, if you know the author or title of one book on the subject you are interested in, look that up in the Author/Title Catalog and note what subject headings were assigned. These will guide you to correct headings in the Subject Catalog.

Figure 7-2
Library guide. (University of Wisconsin, Madison Memorial Library.)

using the subject catalog

The filing order in the Subject Catalog is briefly as follows:

1.	Subject without subdivision	EDUCATION
2.	With dash and subdivision	
	a. Form or subject subdivisions	EDUCATION - FINANCE
		EDUCATION - STUDY AND TEACHING
	b. Time subdivisions	EDUCATION - 18th CENTURY
		EDUCATION - 19th CENTURY
	c. Place subdivisions	EDUCATION - GERMANY
		EDUCATION - UNITED STATES
3.	With comma and subdivisions	EDUCATION, HIGHER
4.	With parentheses	EDUCATION ( )
5.	Phrase headings	EDUCATION AS A PROFESSION

Sometimes the heading has a subordinate element following a period:

1.	Subject without subdivision	UNITED STATES
2.	With dash and subdivision	UNITED STATES - ANTIQUITIES
3.	With period and subordinate	UNITED STATES. ARMY
4.	Phrase heading	UNITED STATES IN ART

If you have questions about the use of the Subject Catalog or the Library of Congress Subject Headings, be sure to ask the information librarian.

using the periodical index

It is impractical to make subject cards for articles appearing in magazines. However, there are many indexing services which do analyze the subject content of periodicals. Readers Guide to Periodical Literature covers general topics; and there are many specialized indexes, such as Business Periodicals Index. Indexes are located in the Reference Room (262). Ask the reference staff for assistance in finding pertinent indexes or look in the Subject Catalog under the form heading "BIBLIOGRAPHY" following the subject heading, e.g. HISTORY - BIBLIOGRAPHY.

government documents

Government documents are an important source of information of an enormous variety of subjects. Most Federal and Wisconsin state documents are located in the Historical Library, where a document librarian will help you locate materials. The index to U.S. documents, the Monthly Catalog, has a subject index at the end of each issue and an annual cumulation in the December issue. It is located in Reference and at the Historical Library.

Most foreign documents are located in Memorial Library. Some can be found in the card catalog by looking under the name of the country and issuing agency. For others, especially United Nations and British documents, special indexes in the Reference area provide better access. If you don't find what you want, go to the document librarian in Room 262E.

computer searches

Computer searches of social science indexing services are available in the Reference Department of Memorial Library. Searches of other subject areas can be arranged at the Agriculture and Life Science Library (Steenbock), the Health Sciences Library and the Engineering Library.

FOR MORE INFORMATION ON CONDUCTING SUBJECT SEARCHES, CONSULT THE LIBRARIANS IN THE REFERENCE ROOM.

Figure 7-2 (Continued)

to find a periodical

Memorial Library subscribes to the major periodicals in the humanities and social sciences. Current issues of the more heavily used periodicals are located in the Periodical Room (210). Unbound issues of others and all bound volumes are in the Stacks.

finding the call number

Two sources may be consulted to determine the call number and location of a periodical:

The Card Catalog (Room 224): This is the most complete record of periodicals in the University Library system. Most periodicals are listed under title (not the author or title of an individual article), e.g. Journal of American Psychology. Those which have the name of an organization in the title are usually listed under the organization's name, e.g.

> American Society for Information Science
> Journal

Note the call number and location. If the card is stamped University Library or has no designation the periodical is in the Stacks. Cards stamped "Current Numbers in Periodical Room" indicate that recent unbound issues (usually for the current year) are located in Room 240.

The UW Union Catalog of Serials: This printed catalog is a partial listing of periodicals, annuals, and monographic series received by the libraries in the University system. It excludes most periodicals no longer being received and the holdings of the Medical and Library School libraries. Listings from the Law and Historical libraries are currently being added. Copies of this catalog may be found at all public service desks and in the South Stack lounges. Patrons can often save steps by consulting the UW Serials first, but if the title is not listed there, use the card catalog.

library holdings

The catalog card gives information about volumes of a periodical which the Library owns. More precise information regarding receipt of individual issues can be obtained at the Current Serials Record Window. Information about monographic series can also be obtained there.

stack locations

Use the Stack Guides, posted throughout the building, to find out where the periodical is located. Most periodicals are given a call number beginning with AP and are shelved in the South Stacks on levels 1, 1M, and 2M. The arrangement is alphabetical by title, so the periodical often may be found without first obtaining the call number. There are exceptions, however, so this shortcut may not be successful. Note that oversized journals are in a separate alphabet on 2M South.

For assistance, inquire at the Information Desk in the Catalog Room. The librarian also has additional listings of periodicals available at other local libraries.

if you can't find it

If a periodical volume is not on the shelf, several steps may be taken:

1. Search the shelving room across from the elevators where books waiting to be re-shelved are stored.
2. Inquire at the Circulation Desk to see if the volume has been checked out or is at the bindery.
3. Consult the Card Catalog or UW Serials List for duplicate copies.

Figure 7-3
Library guide. (University of Wisconsin, Madison Memorial Library.)

examples of periodical cards

Journals change their names, cease and resume publication, merge and separate, and in general undergo many transmutations. Occasionally two journals may have the same title and can be distinguished only by other information on the catalog card. For these reasons it is advisable to read periodical cards carefully and to examine cards filed on either side of the title sought to be sure you have complete and correct information.

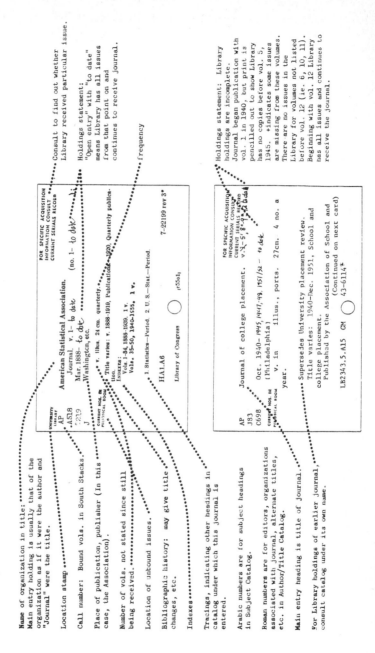

Name of organization in title: Main entry holding is usually that of the organization as if it were the author and "Journal" were the title.

Location stamp

Call number: Bound vols. in South Stacks.

Place of publication, publisher (In this case, the Association).

Number of vols. not stated since still being received.

Location of unbound issues.

Bibliographic history: may give title changes, etc.

Indexes

Tracings, indicating other headings in catalog under which this journal is entered.

Arabic numbers are for subject headings in Subject Catalog.

Roman numbers are for editors, organizations associated with journal, alternate titles, etc. in Author/Title Catalog.

Main entry heading is title of Journal.

For Library holdings of earlier journal, consult catalog under its own name.

Consult to find out whether Library received particular issue.

Holdings statement: "Open entry" with "to date" means Library has all issues from that point on and continues to receive journal.

frequency

Holdings statement: Library holdings are incomplete. Journal began publication with vol. 1 in 1940, but print is pencilled out to show Library has no copies before vol. 5, 1945. +indicates some issues are missing from these volumes. There are no issues in the Library for volumes not listed before vol. 12 (ie. 6, 10, 11). Beginning with vol. 12 Library has all issues and continues to receive the journal.

UNIVERSITY LIBRARY
AP
A518
.229
J

FOR SPECIFIC ACQUISITION INFORMATION CONSULT CURRENT SERIALS RECORD

American Statistical Association.
  Journal. v. 1- to date   (no. 1- to date)
  Mar. 1888- to date
  Washington, etc.
    v. illus. 24 cm. quarterly.
  Title varies: v. 1888-1919, Publications. 1920, Quarterly publication.
  Indexes:
    Vols. 1-34, 1888-1939. 1 v.
    Vols. 35-50, 1940-1955. 1 v.

  1. Statistics—Period. 2. U.S.—Stat.—Period.

HA1.A6   7-22199 rev 3*
Library of Congress   [t5501]

AP
J83
C698

FOR SPECIFIC ACQUISITION INFORMATION CONSULT CURRENT SERIALS RECORD
v. 1- 5, 8-9, 12 to date

Journal of college placement.
  v. 1- Oct. 1940- 1945, 1947, '49, 1951/52- to date
  [Philadelphia]
    v. in illus., ports. 27cm. 4 no. a year.

  Supersedes University placement review.
  Title varies: 1940-Dec. 1951, School and college placement.
  Published by the Association of School and college placement.
                              (Continued on next card)

LB2343.5.A15 CM   43-6114*

Figure 7-3 (*Continued*)

lead you to other resources. Or if your topic deals with personnel practices followed in business, talking with a personnel director in a local business will likely give you invaluable information.

SUMMARY

In this chapter we've mentioned the importance of finding out what resources are available to you on most college and university campuses, what you can expect from these resources, and how you can use the resources to help you with your academic questions and problems.

You and your experiences provide one of the most important resources. Other students are also valuable.

Your major professor or adviser, class instructors, and other professors and staff persons at your school can provide you with invaluable assistance.

Helping centers are available at all colleges and universities and deal with such topics as study skills, writing, reading, and general counseling. Many schools now have special helping centers for the mature adult returning to school.

Libraries are one of the most useful of resources, although it does take some time to get acquainted with what resources are available in libraries and how one goes about obtaining them.

Bookstores and agencies, institutions, and businesses in the community can be valuable resources, particularly if you are dealing with academic questions that have immediate application to practical situations. Often examples of how theories and concepts studied in the classroom are applied can be obtained by interviewing persons in agencies and businesses in the community.

REFERENCES

1 Jean Key Gates, *Guide to the Use of Books and Libraries*, McGraw-Hill, New York, 1974, pp. 61–71.
2 Ibid.
3 Clifford T. Morgan and James Deese, *How to Study*, McGraw-Hill, New York, 1969, p. 89.
4 Ibid., p. 90.
5 Gates, op. cit., pp. 76–81.

CHAPTER 8

FOR THE NEW
GRADUATE STUDENT

If you are one of the many returning students enrolling in a graduate program, this chapter is written specifically for you.

In a few short pages, we couldn't begin to discuss the skills necessary to successfully complete a graduate degree even if we knew all of them. We do plan, though, to share some ideas that many graduate students say are helpful to them as they begin to work on their graduate-degree programs.

Because there are several rather basic differences between undergraduate and graduate programs, the first section of this chapter includes questions to help you understand the graduate program in which you plan to enroll.

The remainder of the chapter focuses on planning a graduate program, preparing a research proposal, and taking graduate examinations. It is in these three areas that many graduate students have problems.

Of course the rest of the book, in which we focus on basic study skills such as reading, writing, and thinking, has application to graduate students as well as to all other students.

In this chapter we will refer to the two basic degrees offered by many graduate schools, the master's degree and the doctor of philosophy degree (Ph.D.). Not all graduate schools offer both degrees, however. Some offer only graduate degrees at the master's level.

The term *master's degree* will refer to all master's degree programs, recognizing that requirements vary considerably from master's program to master's program. For instance, the University of Wisconsin-Madison offers the following master's degrees: master of arts, master of science, master of business administration, master of music, and master of fine arts.

In addition to or in place of it, some graduate programs offer a doctor of education degree that is very similar to the doctor of philosophy. Technically the doctor of education degree is a professional doctorate similar in purpose to the doctor of medicine, doctor of laws, doctor of dental surgery, etc. The professional degree is awarded to those preparing to practice in a particular profession.

Following are questions designed to help you become acquainted with graduate-degree programs.

UNDERSTANDING A GRADUATE-DEGREE PROGRAM

1   What Is the Philosophy of the Department?

For example, if you are seeking admission to a psychology department, is the department's focus primarily clinical or primarily experimental? Are the department and its program traditional or nontraditional, general or specialized? What you must do is attempt to match your interests with the philosophy of the department in which you plan to do graduate work.

2   What Jobs Are Available for Graduates?

Are graduates of the department's program able to obtain jobs in the area of their training? What percentage of last year's graduates who were seeking jobs obtained employment? What are examples of jobs recent graduates have obtained? What are salary ranges? Are these jobs similar to what you expect to do once you've completed the program?

3   What Are the Entrance Requirements?

Most graduate programs review all or most of the following when considering a student for graduate work: undergraduate grade point average (often requiring 2.75 or above, on a 4-point system), satisfactory score on the Graduate Record Examination (GRE) and on the Miller Analogies Test, positive letters of recommendation from persons who know the academic potential of the prospective graduate student, above-average grades on postbachelor's work, and satisfactory completion of a test of writing ability (required for certain social science Ph.D. programs).

Many students who finished their undergraduate programs 10 or more years ago have inadequate undergraduate grade point averages. If this is your case, find out if the graduate school will allow you to enter on academic probation or enroll as a special student until you are able to establish a record of successful work with graduate level courses.

If you plan to enroll in a graduate program different from your undergraduate major, find out if you can take certain deficiency courses to prepare you for graduate work in the department. If your choice of graduate program is far different from your undergraduate work, you should probably pursue another undergraduate degree and consider doing graduate work some time in the future. Returning adults are pursuing second undergraduate degrees in a variety of academic areas.

4 What Is the Entrance Procedure?

How will the decision be made about your admittance to the graduate program you have chosen? Will you have an opportunity to appear in person before an admissions committee to explain your interest in graduate work and your work experience and training? How long will it take for a decision on your admission? If all your materials are in order, a decision should be made and communicated to you within 6 weeks.

5 What Are the Requirements of the Graduate Program?

Requirements will of course vary from program to program, but most graduate programs have several requirements in common. Most require that you maintain a grade point average of B or better in your graduate courses. Most require a minimum residency before a graduate degree will be awarded. For instance, the University of Wisconsin-Madison graduate school requires 36 weeks of residence for the master's degree and 108 weeks of residence for the doctorate. Two weeks of residence credit is granted for each hour of graduate credit completed satisfactorily during a semester. No more than 18 weeks of residence credit may be earned in any one semester. (*Residence* does not mean physical presence on campus. Most departments accept off-campus course work as contributing to residence requirements.) These are minimum requirements established by the graduate school, and various departments have requirements that exceed these.

Find out how much of your graduate program may be earned at other institutions and how much of it may be earned through part-time study. Again using the University of Wisconsin-Madison graduate school as an example, students enrolled in the doctor of philosophy program must spend a minimum of "one continuous academic year in the major field beyond the master's level as a full-time graduate student, carrying a full load of graduate course work or research, and must devote one's self entirely to the graduate program."[1] For the total graduate program, at least half of the residence credit must be earned from graduate work taken on the Madison campus.

What graduate courses are required for the degree you are pursuing? Some programs offer considerable flexibility in course selection; others are quite restricted.

Are foreign languages required? Many graduate departments require reading competency in at least two foreign languages. The reason for this requirement is that students will be able to read research reports in the original language.

Is a minor required? Many graduate programs, particularly those at the doctoral level, require students to have a concentration of course work (a minor) in an area outside their major. This requirement, usually about 10 to 12 semester credits, is determined by the department in which the student wishes to minor. Many graduate schools also allow students who want a broader minor to do their minor course work in more than one department.

What is the research requirement? At most institutions, the graduate degree is a research degree. This is particularly so at the doctoral level. Even when the graduate degree does not have a heavy research focus— the case with some professional master's degree programs—some research requirement is still present.

At the doctor of philosophy level, the research requirement may involve taking courses in statistics, computer science, and research methodology and completing a dissertation. The *dissertation* is a report of original research completed by the student and is usually seen as the capstone of the student's doctoral program. At many graduate institutions, students invest more time in carrying out and reporting their research than they do in taking course work.

At the master's level, students sometimes have the option of writing a master's thesis. The alternative is to do what is sometimes called a *degree in course*, or a professional degree that puts less emphasis on carrying out original research and more emphasis on completing courses. This alternative is particularly attractive to students who do not wish to pursue the doctorate when they complete the master's.

What comprehensive examinations are required? A major difference between an undergraduate and a graduate degree is the increased emphasis on analysis and integration. Comprehensive examinations are designed to measure the extent to which graduate students are able to analyze and integrate what they have been studying. At the master's level usually an oral or a written examination is required at the end of the program. At the doctoral level, the comprehensive examination, which is usually called the *preliminary examination* (prelim.), is given when the student's course work for the program is completed. A doctoral student is not officially admitted to candidacy for the doctorate until the student has passed the comprehensive preliminary examination in the major field.

Besides passing the comprehensive examination, a doctoral student is required to defend a dissertation in a final oral examination. This is usually a 2-hour examination in which the student meets with his or her five-person graduate committee.

6 How Are Graduate Programs Planned?

As mentioned above, some graduate programs have considerable flexibility in the courses that a student will take. How much input will you have in determining your courses? To what extent will your graduate program be the result of discussions between you and your major professor—a rather ideal situation for most graduate students? Will you be able to plan your graduate program so you can determine the time it will take to complete all the requirements?

7 What Is the Minimum and Maximum Credit Enrollment during Any Semester?

To plan the time required for your total program with some accuracy you must know how many credits to take each semester. Some institutions restrict total credits to 12 per semester, with a minimum of 2 credits for the part-time student.

If you are working full time you will likely take less than a full-time credit load. If, however, you have a 20-hour-per-week graduate assistantship, most institutions require you to take a full-time study load—a minimum of 9 credits.

8 How Are Major Professors Selected?

Whether you are a master's degree or a doctoral degree candidate, you will work closely with your major professor. You need to find out how this person is selected and whether you will have any voice in the selection.

In many departments a temporary adviser is assigned to all new graduate students. After a time, up to a semester, a permanent assignment is made. You should have an opportunity to select your major professor, as you will spend many hours working with this person, particularly if you are a doctoral student. The temporary-adviser concept is helpful, for it gives you time to get to know the faculty in the department before selecting a permanent major professor.

In some instances you may want to select your permanent major professor before enrolling in a graduate program. You may know a professor in your field of interest whom you respect and with whom you want to do graduate work. But consider the practical problem of work load. The professor of your choice may not have time to add one more graduate student to an already heavy advising load.

9   How Are Graduate Committees Formed?

In most graduate programs, the overall direction for a student's research and sometimes course selection as well is the responsibility of a graduate committee chaired by the student's major professor. At the master's level the committee usually consists of two persons plus the major professor. At the doctoral level the committee usually includes five persons. One is the major professor, one represents the minor field of study, and there are three other professors. Three persons from the committee make up the preliminary examination committee: they have the responsibility for writing and evaluating this examination. Three persons from the committee—who may be the same as the preliminary examination committee—serve on the dissertation committee. This three-person committee has the responsibility for working closely with the student from the beginning of the research project to the completion of the dissertation. The major professor chairs both the preliminary examination committee and the dissertation committee.

The entire five-person committee conducts the final oral examination, in which the doctoral student defends his or her dissertation.

Do you have input in selecting the members of your graduate committee, with the assistance of your major professor? In most graduate programs this is the case. Graduate students who have been in a department for a time know which professors are interested in their research and which professors work well with each other.

10   What Financial Aids Are Available?

Most adults returning to school need financial assistance. In most graduate departments there are available three kinds of assistantships: research assistantships, project assistantships, and teaching assistantships. All of these are usually 20 hours per week. As the title suggests, the research assistant assists a professor with research. Usually the student is also able to do personal research as part of the assistantship, thus not only receiving financial aid but also obtaining financial help for doing the research required by the degree program. Project assistants may work for the departmental secretary, being responsible for various administrative tasks, or they assist with any of a variety of programs conducted by the department. Occasionally, graduate students are able to obtain project assistantships in other university units, such as university extension. Teaching assistantships involve responsibility for conducting discussion sections of a lecture course and perhaps even giving an occasional lecture in the absence of the professor. The teaching assistant works closely with the course professor, assisting with the planning and carrying out of a course, including the administration and grading of examinations.

Not only do assistantships provide financial help to the student, but they also provide a type of internship experience that is of great value to most students. Working side by side with a professor on a research project or with a professor teaching a course provides an opportunity that is different from that provided in learning opportunities such as lectures, discussions, and so on.

Also available to returning graduate students are scholarships, fellowships, and loans. Inquire at the graduate school where you enroll for more information.

11 What Are the Characteristics of Other Graduate Students in the Program?

One of the greatest resources to any graduate student is the other graduate students enrolled in the program. Before enrolling in a program ask to meet some of the graduate students already there. What are their interests? What kinds of research projects are they pursuing? What are their attitudes toward the graduate program in the department? What are their attitudes toward the faculty? What are their backgrounds? How old are they? Are many of them returning students like yourself? Do they appear to be helping each other in courses and research projects?

12 How Are Graduate Students Involved in Departmental Decision Making?

Do graduate students serve on the department's committees, such as the graduate admissions committee, the graduate program committee, and the examinations committee? Do graduate students have a say in what new courses will be offered by the department and which courses will be eliminated? Do graduate students have a voice in making adjustments in graduate-degree requirements? Do graduate students have an input into what the admissions requirements for the department will be? Are graduate students asked to help evaluate faculty?

TIPS FOR PLANNING A GRADUATE-STUDY PROGRAM

Assuming you will have a considerable voice in determining the content of your graduate-study program, what are some approaches you might use in planning?

First, it is essential that you have a clear idea of your overall study goals. You must be able to answer the questions, Why are you pursuing a graduate degree? and What do you hope to do when you complete your degree? Many returning students are seeking an advancement in their present career or are changing careers. A few persons are enrolled in graduate-degree programs for the self-improvement opportunities such programs offer, with no particular career plans in mind.

If you are having problems with goal setting, the following references may be helpful:

Bolles, Richard Nelson: *What Color Is Your Parachute: A Practical Manual for Job-Hunters and Career Changers,* Ten Speed Press, Berkeley, Calif., 1980.

Campbell, David: *If You Don't Know Where You're Going, You'll Probably End Up Somewhere Else,* Argus, Niles, Ill., 1974.

Crystal, John C. and Richard N. Bolles: *Where Do I Go from Here with My Life?* Seabury, New York, 1974.

Once you know your overall goals, the next logical question is, How do you plan to meet those goals? For most graduate programs, the core learning opportunities are courses and research, supplemented by independent-study work, internships, and the like. As mentioned above, some graduate programs at the master's level are focused almost entirely on course work and have little or no research requirement.

Selecting courses for a graduate program can be trying. Start with the graduate catalog, which lists all the courses offered. But be careful. Courses change over the years as different professors teach them and even as the same professors teach them. Often the course descriptions outlined in graduate catalogs have not kept up with the actual content of the courses.

To solve this problem, contact the professor who teaches the course. Ask for a copy of the course outline, and if you have questions, discuss them with the professor responsible for the course.

Another way to learn about the content of a course is to talk with students who have recently taken the course. They can not only tell you about the course's content, but they can also give you an evaluation of the quality of the course and the professor teaching it.

A third way to learn about courses is to talk with your major professor. He or she, however, cannot have as much information about the content of the course as the students who have recently taken it or the professor who teaches it.

Also, in deciding on possible courses to take, find out when the courses are offered. Often one course is a prerequisite to another. You need to know the semesters when courses are offered to plan courses in sequence.

Because many persons are pursuing graduate course work on a part-time basis, you need to find out when courses are taught during the day. Many graduate departments are now offering courses during the evening or late afternoon particularly to accommodate those persons who are working full time.

Occasionally graduate courses are offered away from campus, as a service to persons living in a community that is too far away from the campus for commuting. Find out if such courses are available in your graduate program.

Most graduate departments allow you to transfer courses into your graduate program from other institutions. Are courses that will fit your graduate program available to you in your community but offered by another college? And will these credits transfer into your graduate program?

Will you be able to design independent-study opportunities in those areas that interest you but for which no courses are available?

Once you know the courses that are available, the content of these courses, and the time they are taught, you are now able, with your major professor, to plan your graduate-study program.

One final consideration that many students overlook is developing a close relationship between the planned course work and the research problem that they will pursue. Some students come to a graduate department with a research idea clearly in mind. They, of course, can rather easily guide their course selection to relate to their research. Other students come to graduate programs with no idea whatever of what research problem to pursue.

Without question, the closer a student's course work can relate to research interest the easier will be the research activity. The amount of time spent on a research project will often be decreased as well, as much of the background reading for the research is done as the student reads for the various courses.

This means, then, that the graduate student should attempt to define a research topic as soon as possible after beginning a graduate program. For the full-time master's degree student this usually means during the first semester of study. For the full-time doctoral student, sometime during the first year of study is a reasonable time to define a research topic.

TIPS FOR PREPARING A RESEARCH PROPOSAL

Planning, conducting, and writing up the results of a research project are part of most graduate-degree programs. This requirement is part of all doctoral programs and is part of most master's degree programs as well.

The research proposal, a written document prepared by the graduate student, is the tool used to communicate to the student's graduate committee the plans for a research project.

How does one go about preparing such a proposal and what are the component parts?

1   The Proposal Should Represent a Research Interest of the Student.

Because you will spend many hours on your research project, from the development of a proposal to the writing of the thesis or dissertation, the topic must be of considerable interest to you. The problem you plan to research should be one that you believe will make a contribution to knowledge and/or will help solve some practical problem. You must believe in the importance of the project.

You may, however, select a research topic and find out, once you begin the research, that the project isn't as important or as interesting as you originally thought. If this is the case, select another topic.

Realistically speaking you will find, though, that even with a project in which you have high general interest there will be times when you will be bored, upset, or disappointed. This is a reaction that all researchers experience at one time or another. You must be able to know the difference between a project that has completely lost your interest and one in which there are some of the problems and disappointments that come with most research efforts.

2   The Research Project Should Be of Interest to and within the Competency of Your Major Professor.

If your major professor has little interest and/or competency in the research topic you wish to pursue, then all things being equal, you should find another major professor.

Ideally, you want a major professor with research interests that are similar to yours. Often it is possible to tie your research interest into an ongoing research project conducted by your major professor. In this way students are often able to obtain funding for carrying on their personal research while they are assisting their major professor with his or her overall research efforts.

3   Teaming with Other Graduate Students Can Provide Dividends in Conducting Research.

A fringe benefit of getting to know the other graduate students in the department and their research interests is the possibility of doing team research. Team research is where two or more graduate students work together on the same large research project. Each graduate student identifies a piece of research that he or she works on, yet there is a relationship of the individual pieces to the larger research project.

Often funded research projects under the direction of one or more professors are carried out this way.

Some definite advantages result from a team effort. Often students can work together in collecting data. Travel expenses as well as computer, clerical, and other expenses can be shared under this arrangement. Students working together can often challenge each other through informal discussions that will strengthen the individual student's research as well as enhance the overall research project.

The psychological benefit that results when several students are working together on a project cannot be overlooked. When students experience problems with their individual research, and they do, they have someone with whom they can share their concerns.

Likewise, when the project is going well they have someone with whom they can share their joy. Interaction resulting from both positive and negative concerns can maintain the individual's motivation toward working on a research project.

4 Use Common Sense When Considering the Scope of Graduate Research.

Many students begin their research plans with project ideas that would take 5 years and a million dollars to complete. One of the steps in the selection of a research project is to be realistic about the time you have for the completion of your project and the amount of financial resources you have.

Often your major professor, because he or she has worked with many students and many research projects, can help you make realistic plans for your research. Other students who are in the midst of or near the completion of their research can help you assess the reality of your research ideas in terms of actually carrying out the research.

5 Avoid Unquestioningly Accepting Available Data for Your Research.

Often, particularly if a department has several ongoing research projects, there will be leftover data that are available for students to use. There are times when using such data can be an extremely efficient and inexpensive way for a student to develop a research project. But doing this can be a dangerous trap. The student is enticed by having data easily available and doesn't first think about a problem to be researched. In effect the student begins a research project with answers for which there are no questions. If, however, the student's research problem can be answered with these available data, by all means the student should use them. The key, though, is to begin the development of a research proposal with a research problem or question rather than beginning with research data in search of a problem.

6 Avoid Designing a Research Project around a Favorite Research Instrument or a Favored Research Approach.

Occasionally a graduate student will discover a research instrument, such as an interview schedule, that has considerable appeal. The student then sets out to design a research proposal based on that instrument. This is an error, unless of course the purpose of the student's research is to refine and further develop the research instrument.

When a student begins a research proposal with a specific research instrument in mind, the problems are similar to those of beginning with available data. Unless the research problem is carefully defined, there are usually difficulties. Once a research problem is defined, the student usually discovers that the original interesting instrument is not the one that will help most in collecting data for the research project.

Likewise, some graduate students begin the development of their research with a given approach to research in mind. For instance, they may want only to do experimental research or they may be interested only in participant observation research or survey research. As in the example above, these students are beginning in the wrong place. The nature of the research problem identified will often suggest the most appropriate research approaches to follow. Again, the place to start is with the research problem.

How to Prepare the Research Proposal

Though research proposals will vary as research topics vary, most graduate research proposals contain the following basic components.

Research Proposal Outline

1 *Introduction* One or two general paragraphs that indicate the nature of the research problem and the objectives of the research. This allows the reader to put the entire research proposal into perspective.

2 *Background Statement* A brief description of the information related to the research problem area. Depending on the topic, this may be a discussion of an important issue or theory in the field or a description of the history, setting, program, or situation leading to the research problem. The purpose of this section is to set the stage for the discussion of the specific problem.

3 *Statement of the Research Problem* A clear statement of the specific problem to be investigated. Often a series of questions is the best way to summarize this section.

4 *Theoretical Framework* A brief description of the history related to the research; the relationship between the proposed study and the theory should be clearly indicated. For instance, hypotheses usually relate directly to the theory. (Not all proposed research has a theory that relates to it.)

5 *Objectives and/or Hypotheses* Often this section includes a general statement giving the main purpose of the study. This is followed by specific objectives and/or hypotheses. Depending on the nature of the study, either objectives, hypotheses, or both may be used.

6 *Assumptions* If the proposed study has inherent assumptions, these should be noted briefly.

7 *Procedures to Be Used*

a *Sources of data and sampling* If a sample is to be used, a description of the procedure that will be followed in drawing the sample.

b *Instrumentation* An outline of the instruments that will be used for collecting data and a description of the instruments if they are available. If not available, a description of the procedures for developing the instruments.

c *Data collection* An outline of the general plan for collecting data which includes a brief timetable.

d *Data analysis* A description of statistical and/or other analysis procedures to be used in achieving the objectives of the study or testing the hypotheses.

e *Data presentation* A plan for how the data will be presented. A description of how the data will be used to meet objectives of the study.

8 *Significance of the Study* An indication of the theoretical and/or practical contributions of the study.

9 *Definition of Terms* Definitions of important concepts and unfamiliar terms used in the study.

10 *Bibliography* A listing of writings used in the development of the proposal.[2]

TIPS FOR TAKING GRADUATE EXAMINATIONS

Within a graduate program there are three levels of examinations beyond those that are part of normal course work: (1) entrance examinations, (2) comprehensive examinations, and (3) research defense examinations.

Entrance Examinations

Entrance examinations, as mentioned above, often include the Graduate Record Examination, the Miller Analogies Test, and examinations designed to test a prospective graduate student's ability to write. Refer to Chapter 2 for references that will help in preparing you for the GRE and the Miller Analogies Test.

The test of writing ability, often administered to prospective doctoral-level graduate students, takes several forms. One common form is a 4-hour examination in which the prospective student selects an issue and then takes a position on it. The test measures the student's ability to take a position on an issue and defend it by following acceptable standards for writing English prose. The evaluators of the examination are not so interested in the details—the facts that are presented—as they are interested in how the argument is developed and how well the student is able to defend a position. Usually a committee of faculty, such as a graduate admissions committee, is responsible for reading and evaluating tests of writing ability.

Comprehensive Examinations

As the title suggests, comprehensive examinations are designed to measure the extent to which a graduate student is able to integrate into a whole all the material studied during a graduate program.

In a master's program the comprehensive examination comes at the end of the program. In a doctoral program the comprehensive examination, usually referred to as the *comprehensive preliminary examination,* comes at the end of the course work. For most doctoral students this is usually about halfway through the doctoral program, for considerable time is usually necessary to complete the research requirement of the program after the course work has been completed.

Comprehensive examinations may take several forms. They may be open-book, take-home examinations with a deadline of, say, 5 days to complete. They may be sit-down, classroom-type examinations in which a student writes for 4 hours or sometimes much more—up to 2 days or 16 hours—without any notes or references. Often the comprehensive examination is oral in nature and the student is examined by his or her graduate committee for from 2 to 4 hours.

It is not unusual for the comprehensive examination to be some combination of the above forms. Part of the examination may be a take-home section, which is then followed by an oral examination. Part of the examination may be take-home, and part may be sit-down and traditional in nature. Part may be traditional sit-down, and part may be 2-hour oral.

In some graduate departments students have a voice as to the form of comprehensive examination they will take. Some students prefer an oral examination, while others prefer a traditional sit-down one. Many prefer the open-book, take-home type of examination. In some graduate departments the student and the student's graduate committee together decide on the form the comprehensive examination will take.

Tips for Preparing for and Taking Comprehensive Examinations   Refer to Chapter 2, to the discussion on essay and oral examinations, for some ideas that apply to comprehensive examinations. Here are some additional ideas that graduate students have found helpful.

1 When reviewing all the materials presented in the course work that was part of the graduate program, try to select the big ideas or major concepts presented. Using the big-idea approach, on note cards filed together according to major ideas write supporting information that may have been presented in several courses.

2 Avoid going back to do extensive reading as part of the review process. This type of reading sometimes can be more confusing than enlightening. At the review stage for a comprehensive examination you are concerned with integrating all that you have learned so far. Often additional details obtained from reading at this stage in your program get in the way of the integration process.

3 For many fields of study, particularly in the social sciences, another useful approach is to identify major issues in the field and then attempt to determine your position on these issues and the evidence you would use to support your position.

4 Studying with other graduate students who are also preparing for comprehensive examinations can be extremely useful. This process works best when students give each other assignments to lead discussions and raise questions.

5 Each student, although involved in a group-study program, must also review alone. Often the group study will help you identify areas where you need to do more thinking.

6 Start the review process well ahead of the time when you will take the comprehensive examination. At the doctoral level many students begin their review 6 months before they take the examination. At the master's level this time is shorter, say, 2 months. But reviewing for a comprehensive examination is not done in a week.

7 During the review process, study old examinations. Write practice answers to examination questions and then let your fellow students evaluate your answers.

8 As you review, make certain that the answers you prepare are your own, not quotations from books and other authorities you have read. One of the most serious shortcomings of students who write comprehensive examinations is to string together quotation after quotation without demonstrating any real ability to integrate ideas. Sometimes students reviewing for the comprehensive examination fail to understand the difference between using quotations from authorities to answer questions and using quotations from authorities to support their (the students') answers to the questions. Those evaluating comprehensive examinations are concerned first with a student's ability to answer questions and take positions and second with the student's ability to recite literature and the research of various authorities.

9 For the written comprehensive examination, follow the suggestions in Chapter 2 for writing the essay examination. Spend up to 10 percent of the time you have for the examination outlining and planning your answers.

10 For the oral comprehensive examination, refer to the section on oral examinations in Chapter 2 for suggestions.

Preparing for and Taking Research Defense Examinations

Graduate students, at both the master's and the doctoral levels, who have research requirements as part of their graduate programs usually are required to defend their research in a final oral examination. For most graduate students, the oral defense of their thesis or dissertation is the culmination of their graduate program, the last activity before they are granted their graduate degrees.

Some students find this an extremely anxiety-laden situation, worrying about their graduate committee's questions and their ability to answer them. The situation is potentially stressful because there are usually five people asking in-depth questions about your research for at least an hour and usually 2 hours.

Often, though, the extreme stress shown by some students as they prepare for their final orals is unfounded. Let's look at the situation. You the graduate-student researcher have worked on your research project for a considerable time, at least 2 years or longer if you are a Ph.D. student. You know more about your research than any member of your committee does. You've done the background reading, you've studied the related theory, you know your data, you've wrestled with the analysis of your data, and you've thought long about the implications and conclusions of your work. You have every reason to go into an oral examination with confidence—not arrogance but confidence.

Also, you've already spent many hours working with your dissertation committee: with individual members and with the entire committee.

Committee members have likely raised many questions while you worked on your paper, and you have tried to satisfy their concerns insofar as possible. When you come to the oral examination you should be reasonably assured that at least three members of your oral committee, those who were your dissertation committee, are in agreement with you and are on your side.

The final oral examination is not designed to fail students. After a major professor and a graduate committee have spent hours (years) working with a student, they don't want the student to fail.

What your major professor and the committee do want is as good a piece of research writing as possible. So, often during the final oral will come some additional suggestions for how to improve your thesis or dissertation. These suggestions should be taken not as failures, but as honest shortcomings that befall any researcher. The committee, then, if it operates as do many final oral committees, is a committee of research peers assisting one of their peers in polishing his or her research.

SUMMARY

Though nearly all the study skills discussed so far in this book have application, there are some additional skills graduate students need.

One of the skills is the process for selecting a graduate department in which to study. Some of the questions to ask include:

1 What is the philosophy of the department?
2 What jobs are available for graduates?
3 What are the entrance requirements?
4 What is the entrance procedure?
5 What are the requirements of the graduate program?
6 How are graduate programs planned?
7 What is the minimum and maximum credit enrollment during any semester?
8 How are major professors selected?
9 How are graduate committees formed?
10 What financial aids are available?
11 What are the characteristics of other graduate students in the program?
12 How are graduate students involved in departmental decision making?

Planning your graduate program, including selecting courses and other learning opportunities such as internships and independent study, is one of the most important tasks for a graduate student. This is particularly so in those graduate programs in which there is considerable flexibility and in which students are heavily involved in making decisions about what should be in their graduate programs.

Courses and research are usually the core of most graduate programs. Consultation with your major professor, with a course's instructor, and with students who have taken the course will provide you with information that will help you decide to take or not take a course.

In planning a research proposal, the following suggestions have been found helpful by graduate students:

1 The proposal should represent a research interest of the student.

2 The research project should be of interest to and within the competency of your major professor.

3 Teaming with other graduate students on a research project can provide dividends in conducting research.

4 Use common sense when considering the scope of graduate research.

5 Avoid unquestioningly accepting available data for your research.

6 Avoid designing a research project around a favorite research instrument or a favored research approach.

Most research proposals contain these rather standard components: (1) introduction, (2) background statement, (3) statement of research problem, (4) theoretical framework, (5) objectives and/or hypotheses, (6) assumptions, (7) procedures to be used, (8) significance of the study, (9) definition of terms, (10) bibliography.

Graduate students are asked to take three types of examinations beyond those examinations that are part of regular courses: (1) entrance examinations, (2) comprehensive examinations, and (3) research defense examinations. As with course examinations, there are certain skills necessary for preparing for and taking these examinations.

REFERENCES

1 University of Wisconsin, *Graduate School Social Sciences and Humanities, Bulletin of The University of Wisconsin-Madison,* Madison, Wisc., 1975, p. 10.

2 Adapted from a class handout for 268–601. Research Methods, taught by Mohammad Douglah and later by Chere Coggins, in the department of continuing and vocational education, University of Wisconsin-Madison.

CHAPTER 9

IMPROVING THE SYSTEM

"So old, so old," Irene Kampen's college adviser muttered when he reviewed her transcript, which was 25 years old. She didn't know if the adviser was referring to her or to her transcript. Her account of the problems she encountered as a returning student are at the same time a hilarious and a sad account of one university's response to an older returning student.[1]

Since Ms. Kampen faced her college adviser upon returning to school, several changes have occurred. Older students returning to college are not the oddity they were 10 years ago. Many changes have been made in the organization and operation of colleges and universities to accommodate and even, in some instances, encourage the older student who returns to college. But many more changes are necessary.

Harrington points out that even today many students returning to college face comments like: "Do you mean you didn't go to college at all? Why did you wait all these years before applying?" "I'm sorry, we don't take part-time students."[2]

After the returning student listens for a while, two lines of advice are usually offered: (1) Forget about a degree. Do some reading at home, or maybe sign up for some noncredit extension courses. (2) If you insist on credit, try evening college or perhaps summer school. How about an extension or a correspondence course?[3]

It is impossible in one short chapter to discuss all the problems that returning students have faced and continue to face when they return to school. And likewise it is impossible here to suggest all the changes that colleges and universities should consider if they want to make their programs attract and meet the needs of the returning student.

We do, however, want to outline some of the problems, and suggest some approaches you the returning student might consider to help correct the situation. Consider what is here a beginning. Much work is needed in this area as colleges and universities adjust to the growing number of older adults returning to campuses to study.

SOME PROBLEM AREAS

Entrance Procedures

The mechanics of registration are a problem for many returning students. Registration hours often conflict with work schedules, and registration often requires traveling to the campus a week or more before classes begin to complete the process. Some colleges are correcting these problems by allowing registration by mail or phone.

Many adults have accumulated college credits at a variety of institutions around the country. Getting these credits accepted by a school in which the student wishes to pursue a degree program is often a problem.

Many returning students bring with them a mediocre record of college work that was completed 10 or more years ago. Many entrance officials continue to place heavy emphasis on these old transcripts when considering students for admission. This is especially so at the graduate level, where considerable emphasis is placed on the undergraduate grade point average for determining admissibility.

Many returning students know they will not be able to complete a degree at a particular institution but want to take courses that will eventually contribute to a degree. They may plan to live in a community for only a few years, not enough time to complete a degree but enough time to take several courses. They are what are commonly referred to today as "stop in" and "stop out" students. But many college entrance officials continue to view these students as dropouts and consider them unfavorably when they apply for admission to a new institution.

Another problem that increasingly appears involves equivalency credit. Returning adults have a variety of experiences gained from their work, community, and social lives. Too often colleges and universities ignore these experiences when considering a student for admission to a college program. As a result many returning adults are forced to take college-level courses for which they already have the content and skills, based on their life experience. Colleges and universities need to work out systems for recognizing the life experiences of returning adult students when determining required courses. Some institutions are beginning with the assumption that a student's competencies, however acquired and as determined through appropriate types of examinations, be used in determining what further requirements are necessary for a degree.

Learning Opportunities

Problems exist at several levels. The opportunities that are made available, the way they are made available, the hours they are available, and the content of these opportunities are all problem areas.

On many campuses the majority of educational opportunities are traditional courses, taught by a professor or a teaching assistant who uses primarily the lecture method of instruction. The courses meet two or three times a week for a 50-minute period or sometimes once a week for a combined 100-minute period. An increasing number of colleges and universitites, however, are offering a variety of educational opportunities in a variety of formats. These include internships, independent-study courses of various types, programmed instruction, seminars, cooperative-study projects in which several students study together, small-group discussions, and student-led discussions, to mention a few.

A postgraduate professional-improvement program conducted at a major university uses the following instructional approaches: (1) a semester of full-time residence instruction, (2) programmed independent study climaxed by a 2-week term in residence, (3) two 8-week or four 4-week terms in residence, (4) once-a-week extension classes in combination with 2-week terms in residence, (5) once-a-month weekend extension or residence seminars in combination with 2-week terms in residence, (6) coordinated combinations of 2, 3, 4, and 5.[4]

Not only are many colleges offering a variety of learning opportunities; they also are offering them at hours and locations that make participation easier for the part-time student. Some universities offer an extended timetable, which means that they make courses available in the late afternoon and early evening. Some institutions offer courses off campus, in the student's community. Others offer courses in weekend formats.

A further problem that many students face is having their entire curriculum dictated to them by various degree requirements. Returning, mature, adult students want a voice in the selection of the courses they will take.

Returning students also want the opportunity to take courses without getting degree credit. They may want to upgrade themselves in their profession or even to change careers. But they often are not interested in obtaining a degree. However, these students do want recognition that they took the courses. One way of doing this is developing post-B.S. and post-M.S. certificate programs.

College Instructors

It is not always the instructors' fault that many of them are problems for returning students. Many instructors work on campuses where obtaining tenure is of the ultimate concern for the first 6 years of their work. And tenure is earned, at many campuses, by scholarly activity as evidenced through publishing, not through teaching and counseling nontraditional or any other kind of student.

Thus the returning student often meets a college instructor whose first allegiance is to research and writing, not to teaching and counseling. Some instructors get so caught up in their scholarly work that they spend the remainder of their academic lives doing what Alexander Mood calls "cathedral building."[5]

Cathedral building, according to Mood, is spending a lifetime researching irrelevant topics that are so narrowly defined that only a handful of persons in the world understand enough of what the researcher is doing to challenge it. And they won't challenge it because they are working on the same irrelevant topic.

Thus students who expect to have instructors interested in them and their learning—who indeed have paid a considerable sum of tuition money with that expectation—often meet extreme lack of interest.

Until the tenure system is modified so that teaching and counseling are recognized as at least equal to scholarly work, this problem will continue. The answer is a balance between scholarship and teaching. It would be as wrong to award tenure only for teaching and counseling performance as it is wrong today to award tenure almost entirely for scholarly achievements.

Many college instructors do not understand adult learners. Many instructors have spent years working with students who have recently graduated from high school, and these instructors are usually unaware that the returning adult student has differing characteristics and needs. In Chapter 1 we discussed several characteristics of the adult learner that are important to consider when developing learning experiences for this student. One obvious and important error that is easily overlooked is to consider a group of students with varying ages as having similar needs and characteristics. In the past, when the group of students included only an age span of 4 years, say, from 19 to 23, this was somewhat possible to do. But it is not possible to do when the age span is 40 years, say, from 19 to 60, and at least two generations.

The attitude that many instructors have toward students is not one that many students can or should accept. Traditionally, a college education was thought of as a preparation for life. One went to college, then entered the world of work and adult life. Returning adult students have already lived a considerable number of years. They may be preparing for a different kind of life—a new career, for example. But on the other hand, these returning students may be interested primarily in improving the careers they have been in for 10 or more years. Many women are returning to school after their children are grown, to pursue a new career outside the home. Some women are returning to school so that they can support themselves rather than be seen as educated helpmates to educated husbands. Many returning students are interested not in preparing for life but in improving the life they are already living, with its many challenges and changes.

Another attitudinal problem concerns the relationship of the college instructor to the student. A returning graduate student, asked about the problems he faced when returning to a college campus, wrote:

I am not allowed to take responsibility for my own actions. As in my childhood my parents took responsibility for me, now my professors watch my behavior and approve the steps I am taking. I am supposed to keep them informed about what I am doing and gain their approval. The relationship might be even closer to that between a physician and a patient. As a patient you keep the physician informed; the doctor listens and, with the help of some additional tests (which you are not supposed to understand), tells you about your status and prescribes your next steps. The doctor is in the possession of some magic knowledge that makes it possible to know what is best for you. Your obedience to the rules is necessary for your health and the doctor's status and power. Only if he or she is willing to give up something of the latter can there be a different relationship and even faster health improvements. The sacred and magical skill of the academic staff is their superior control of the scientific inquiry or research methods. Only the professors know when you perform healthy research. They decide your status or if you possess the potential of becoming healthy. They carry the responsibility for you.

If my perceptions are accurate it means that we do very seldom see an honest and true dialogue between professors and students. The students will be inclined to seek the truth that their professors are assumed to accept. This relationship can become detrimental for both the student and the professor. The professor becomes isolated not only from the society outside the academic world but also from the students.

Others comments included:

Several of my professors are younger than I am. They completed their graduate work without ever working outside the confines of the university. I am a threat to them, both because I am older and because I have had several years of experience in the area we are studying in class. How much better it would be if the professor would relax a little, and allow (even encourage) students who have experiences that are relevant to the content of the course to share them. This would make a richer experience for everyone. We wouldn't lose any respect for the professor and his position either. Quite the contrary, I think many students like me would admire a professor who was smart enough to draw on the experiences of his students to bring theory and practice together. Isn't relating theory and practice to each other one of the reasons many of us are studying at the university?

Another attitude that sometimes gets in the way of a good relationship between returning older students and their instructors is the myth that older students are not serious students. Either it has been forgotten or many professors have never heard about the success of integrating thousands of veterans into colleges and universities at the end of World War II. These veterans were serious students. They studied hard, and they did well. Likewise, today's older students are serious students. They have goals and aspirations, and they see attending college as one way of accomplishing them.

How the returning student's progress is measured is another problem. Many instructors have developed excellent multiple-choice examinations that can be machine graded and that are carefully timed ''so all of the students have an equal chance.''

One has only to be aware of the physiological change in reaction time that occurs with age to deduce that older adults are at a disadvantage in a timed test. It simply takes an older adult longer to answer the questions. Thus the timed test is unfair to the older student in a mixed class of younger and older students.

Returning students want a broader approach to measuring their progress. They are generally not opposed to examinations, but do resent those that are timed. They would also like the opportunity to demonstrate their progress through other written work, such as term papers and reports, and through oral presentations at various times.

Support Services

It is in this area that many campuses are making progress, yet much more needs to be done.

Libraries must be open in the evenings and on weekends so that the part-time student who is also working full time has an opportunity to use these facilities.

Many campuses have developed counseling services for returning adults to help them with program selection, to assist them in adjusting to the campus setting, and to provide help with sharpening study skills that often have not been used for many years.

Many campuses are providing remedial workshops and courses for students who have deficiencies in areas that are prerequisite to other learning opportunities. For example, many adults returning to school have math deficiencies. Some campuses have developed noncredit workshops designed to improve math skills and help overcome math anxiety, a problem that occurs particularly with women but also with many men.

Child care is another problem area. Many campuses have organized day care centers. But many also need to organize drop-in child care centers for the mother who wants to spend a couple of hours at the library and can't find a sitter for such a short time and, usually, on short notice. At the library there could be a drop-in child care facility where the mother could leave her youngster while she studies.

Financial aid for the returning adult, particularly the person who is attending school part time, continues to be a problem on many campuses. Many financial aid programs insist that students study full time before they are eligible for financial assistance. The part-time student, often with a family, mortgage payments, dental bills, and the like, has a great need for financial help. Almost never can such a student turn to his or her parents for help, as is true with many younger students.

There's a larger dimension to this problem too. Many people in our society believe in and support public dollars for the education of youth. This support, with some exceptions, usually extends through the time that a youngster completes high school and continues with some form of post-secondary education. But when someone suggests that the same support be made available to the adult who never went to college as a youth but wants to begin at age 35, there is opposition. Adults should pay entirely for their education, whatever form it takes, is the prevailing attitude. Thus the returning adult who seeks financial assistance faces this larger problem.

Administration

As pointed out above, some adjustments have been made in such administrative areas as registration times and the hours when classes and courses are offered. But many more changes are necessary if colleges and universities are to be places where returning adult students can easily pursue an education.

Residency requirements pose one set of problems. Many campuses insist that students spend part of their study program—usually a sizable part—physically on campus. Often they must be there as full-time students. For example, the Ph.D. program at the University of Wisconsin-Madison campus requires a student to spend 1 continuous year in full-time study on the Madison campus. Many reasons are offered for this requirement. One of the strongest arguments relates to maintaining the quality of the Ph.D. program and is reflected in the following graduate-school statement used to justify full-time study: "Such a period of full-time reading, reflection, study, and research, without the distraction of outside responsibilities, is considered necessary to give the student continuity in this research and to fulfill the spirit and special demands of a Ph.D. degree program."[6]

As powerful an argument as this is, many students, because of time and financial obligations, find it impossible to meet the requirement. The problem to be addressed by graduate faculties, and by graduate students too, is how the values contained in a requirement for continuous study can be maintained or at least not compromised and yet a more flexible attendance schedule can be developed.

The involvement of students in campus decision making is another area where more progress is necessary. Students should be involved in deciding on what courses are taught, what the content of these courses should be, and when these courses are taught. Students should be involved in the evaluation of faculty members, including the decisions about which of them should and should not receive tenure. Students should be involved in making decisions about full-time study requirements, about entrance requirements, and about plans for long-term institutional change.

Some campus administrators are threatened by student involvement, and some even argue that eventually students will take over higher education and control it. That is not what is suggested here. What is suggested is a sharing of decision making among students, faculty, and administration. From a practical perspective, think of the pool of talent represented in a group of students, many of whom have spent more than 10 years working in business, industry, or some profession. These students have had years of experience with decision making; they know the process; they know the problems in trying to do it. Why not take advantage of this talent? Of course the involvement will also assist the students by giving them an internship experience in higher education decision making. So all gain.

Of course one of the great changes many administrators will need to make is in their basic attitude and in the attitude of their faculty toward the returning older student. Unfortunately, some administrators see returning students only as an answer to the problem of dwindling traditional student numbers. They attempt to attract these students to their campuses to keep their student numbers up and their budgets intact. And they make only minimum changes in the organization and operation of their institutions. If the administrators and faculties of colleges and universities want to look to a future of providing quality programs to both the traditional and the new nontraditional students, then considerable changes of the type we have so briefly touched on here must be made. Much more is necessary than simply printing an attractive brochure inviting older students to attend their campuses, setting up a counseling center in an old, unused office, and teaching a few courses in the late afternoon and evening.

WHAT YOU CAN DO

So far we have outlined a number of problems that you as a returning student will likely face when you enroll in academic work. We have also mentioned some of the solutions that many colleges and universities are attempting. But as we mentioned, much more needs to be done. You the returning student can play an important role in making these changes.

An Attitude toward Change

Let's assume that you are enrolled in a degree program on a campus where you see many of the problems we have talked about in this chapter. What are your alternatives? You can drop out of the program. You can complain to your family and to your fellow students but continue to put up with the program. Or you can do something about the problem.

Many returning students were in school in the late 1940s and 1950s. This was a period when students did not question their teachers, when students generally accepted what was offered them. So you probably bring with you the attitude that you should accept and not question. Likewise, many of your professors likely did graduate work during this same 1950s period, and they, too, are a little skittish about students who raise questions. But they have had some experience with them. During the 1960s, many students raised questions about higher education, sometimes violently as in the college riots that took place during those years. The professors had to respond to questioning students. So even though they themselves may have come from a nonquestioning experience as students, they have had experience with students asking questions. Most of them are open enough to attempt to respond intelligently and rationally to questions concerning problems that students face. They are also very busy people, so many of these professors are not going to raise the questions and identify the problems.

If changes are going to be made on many campuses, you the returning student will need to become involved in raising questions, identifying problems, and assisting in working out the solutions to them.

Working Alone

You can follow three strategies that will in many instances cause change: ask, confront, and suggest. And they are very simple. When you don't understand the reason for something, ask. Ask your instructors, ask your academic adviser, ask a counselor, ask a departmental head, ask a dean, but ask. Ask until you receive an answer that you understand.

Often the requirements are not as rigid as they appear. On many campuses there is much more flexibility in the system than most students recognize. Students must clarify the goals they are seeking and then explore alternatives.

On many campuses students are able to design individual majors. On most campuses students are able to adjust course requirements if they will take the time to discuss their concerns and interests with the instructor.

At times you may need to confront your instructors, your major professor, the same persons we mentioned above. If you have the evidence to suggest a position that is in opposition to one held by your instructor, for example, then by all means confront him or her with this evidence.

You can suggest. From your experience and training you may have discovered an approach to doing something which will improve a bad situation. If so, suggest it.

Well and good, you say, but what are my risks when I attempt any of these approaches? Will I not make it difficult for myself, perhaps even cause myself to get a poor grade or worse, if I question, challenge, or suggest?

The answer to those questions is that you stand to gain far more than you will lose from your efforts. As pointed out above, most professors and departments are open to suggestions for improvement, are open to questions that bother you, and even welcome being challenged on matters where you disagree. In fact a growing number of professors and administrators are encouraged by students who have the gumption to want to improve the system. These students are often rewarded for their efforts with complimentary recommendations when they seek employment.

It is unusual professors, a minority on college campuses, who resent suggestions for improving the system. Be encouraged to be assertive.[7] You will be surprised with the openness and the positive response with which most college staff will receive your comments.

Working with Others

Without question, returning students need to make a group effort to deal with many of the far-reaching problems they face on college campuses. Though some progress can be made with specific problems when individuals work alone, the far-reaching problems require group effort.

Students have used a number of strategies for effecting change. They have carried out sit-ins; they have organized and participated in student strikes; they have participated in take-overs; they have effected boycotts. Some of these approaches have been effective. To the contrary, these approaches have occasionally been abortive or have caused alienation among students and between students and faculty.

That is not to say that the more extreme measures are not sometimes appropriate. There may be extreme situations in which they are the only means to effect change. However, we will outline below a process for effecting change that has the potential for accomplishing much without involving many of the problems associated with the more extreme approaches to change.

Where does a group of students focus its attention when it sees problems that directly concern it? Change can occur at two levels. Taylor suggests that the changes be effected where the education is occurring, in the classrooms and with the professors. He suggests that students and faculty collaborate to make the changes and not wait for the institution to change policy.[8]

In addition to organizing to bring pressure on the faculty at the place where instruction is occurring, Mood says students should form a national organization to effect policy change at every level: local, state, and national.[9]

Mood goes on to suggest that students focus on changing the system. Students "must recognize that the desired change refers to changing a system—not a rule, not a practice, not a course, not a person, but a complete system."[10]

For Mood *system* refers to all levels of society that influence policy-making for colleges and universities: state governments, boards of regents, academic senates, university administrations, university departments, tenured faculty, nontenured faculty, nonacademic staff, students, and the general public.

As the process suggested below allows, changes can and should be made at both levels—the classroom action level and the administrative policy level—at the same time.

A Process for Change The process suggested here grows out of the writings of Paulo Freire, a former Brazilian educator who was concerned with effecting change through group action. Persons interested in this process are strongly encouraged to read Freire's book, *Pedagogy of the Oppressed,*[11] to understand the philosophy that undergirds this process. Following are several assumptions on which the process is based: (1) Human beings are free to create (or recreate) their world. Unlike animals, who must adapt to situations to survive, humans have the alternative of attempting to modify their world and themselves. (2) Reflection and action are integral components of a change process. Persons reflect on a situation, then act based on their reflection. When the action is complete there is more reflection, which in turn leads to more action. Thus it is a never-ending process. Action without reflection is misguided; reflection without action is sterile. (3) Interaction among participants is essential to the process. The process is based on a dialogue among participants who question, listen, and challenge—but at the same time develop a trust relationship among themselves. (4) A process for change can be a growth process for those involved. Participants involved in this process can learn a great deal from their efforts. (5) Consciousness raising is a prelude to action. Many persons face problems that they are not totally aware of, or they "feel" a problem but cannot express it. (6) A reflection-action group can function with minimal leadership. A facilitator is necessary to raise questions and generally move the process forward. The group itself takes major responsibility for its reflection and action.

The process involves six questions that can be treated as phases. The first five questions are designed to help a group become conscious of the problems its members face. The sixth question focuses on the anticipated action: What can be done to correct the problem? The first five questions relate to the reflection phase of the process, and the sixth question relates to the action phase.

The questions are these:

1 What brought you to this academic community?
2 What disappointments have you experienced in this academic community?
3 What dynamic historical forces are operating?
4 What are your present feelings?
5 What contradictions do you perceive?
6 What action do you propose we take?

The first question deals with motivations and goals for coming back to school. The second question explores disappointments returning students have experienced. Question 3 opens up the area of the forces that seem to be affecting the situation in which the students find themselves. The traditions of a university's operations are historical forces affecting returning students. Question 4 starts the members of the group in looking at their feelings concerning going to school, particularly in relation to the responses to questions 1 and 2. Question 5 helps the group members focus on the differences between what they expected to find at the university or college and what they did find. And last, question 6, the action question, triggers the group members to look at what action they can take to correct the problem situations they have identified.

A group of ten students met to work through the reflection-action process. All these students were returning graduate students who had worked

5 to 10 years, on the average, since receiving their undergraduate degrees. The group met on three consecutive Wednesdays and always sat in a circle. Each meeting lasted from about 7:30 to 11:00 or 11:30 P.M. Two members of the group served as coordinators. They had experienced a similar process at an earlier time. The first meeting focused on questions 1 and 2. To begin the process, one of the coordinators described Paulo Freire's philosophy about the assumptions of the process. During the actual process, one coordinator served as a moderator, seeking responses from the group members, clarifying opinions, and encouraging dialogue. The second coordinator recorded the responses on a flip chart.

The second meeting proceeded in much the fashion of the first and took the group through question 5.

The third meeting was concerned entirely with question 6, what action the group could take to deal with the contradictions and problems that were identified during the process.

Below is a summary of the students' responses to the six questions.

1 What brought you to this academic community?
  To learn (social involvement for academic growth)
  Need the degree for employment
  Seeking competency
  Acquire a certain life-style (status)
  Something to do in lieu of a job
  To get new ideas and a better background for increased responsibility
  Prevent stagnation in individual position
  Intellectual stimulation
  To escape
  Family pressure
  Self-actualization
  Alternate employment opportunities
  Social pressures
  Necessity of Ph.D. for university position
  Understand social conditions
  Broaden personal perspective
  Novel experience
  The university was close
2 What disappointments have you experienced in this academic community?
  High cost of education
  Pressure of school (exams, deadlines, time, money)
  Institutionalized selfishness (cut off from other people)
  Competition versus cooperation (many students want to compete with each other rather than cooperate)
  Cut off from old friends due to different values

Educational system not as liberal as expected; rigid emphasis on technical and not on critical thinking

No dialogue in graduate school

No time for friends

Too much intellectualization of feelings

Overemphasis on the evaluation of everything

An intellectual rat race

Received poorer grades than expected

3 What dynamic historical forces are operating?

An educational system with a long tradition and history

4 What are your present feelings?

Frustrated

Disillusioned

Feeling of anticipation

5 What contradictions do you perceive?

Emphasis on self-direction vs. institutional framework. (We are supposed to become self-directed learners, yet the institution tells us how, when, what, and where to learn.)

Broadening education, enlarging perspective vs. specialization, cut off from others, lack of empathy for people with differing views (and lack of contact with them)

Hope for increased dialogue with other students and faculty vs. decreased dialogue

Education as life vs. education as preparation for life

Living now vs. fulfilling requirements and then going to work (and living)

Pressure for quality work vs. pressure for quantity of work

6 What action do you propose we take?

First attempt to change graduate requirements for a master's degree research paper[12]

In terms of action, this group of ten students went back to all the graduate students in its department after the three meetings. The students talked with them, explained what they had been doing, and attempted to get the support and assistance of as many students as possible in making changes in the graduate program in their department. As a result of these discussions, small action committees were formed. They were made up of a combination of members of the original reflection-action group and the larger graduate-student body.

When these smaller committees had studied the situation, they went to the departmental administration with specific proposals for change. To the surprise of several committee members, the departmental administration was pleased with the suggestions, and several changes in policy were made during the coming year. Much more work needed to be done, but the students had made considerable progress. They had learned that they could work together to effect change. They were heard. And they were not discriminated against because they were questioning and attempting to change some of the long-standing departmental policies concerning graduate students.

This process of reflection and action described above is but one example of what a group of students might do to effect change. It is by no means the only approach that a group might wish to follow. The list of readings at the end of this chapter contains ideas for other group actions that students might consider.

A POSITIVE NOTE

It is true that many problems exist on campuses which can hinder returning students from having the most satisfactory experience. But as one returning student wrote: "Sure there are going to be problems along the way and certainly some disillusionment. But what about all the rewards—getting your brain in gear again, having the stimulation of contact with fellow students and professors, seeing an 'A' on a paper you've worked hard on, feeling that you're accomplishing a personal goal."

SUMMARY

In brief overview this chapter introduces several of the problem areas that returning students may face. Many institutions are actively working on these problems as increasing numbers of older students return to college campuses around the country. But much more work is necessary. Problems were discussed in five areas: entrance procedures, learning opportunities, college instructors, support services, and administration.

Two broad approaches for taking action were presented, those strategies individuals can follow by themselves and those approaches that relate to group effort. A case example of action by a group of returning students who used a process based on Paulo Freire's philosophy was presented.

Students should be involved in making decisions about those aspects of campus life that directly affect them. If this involvement is not encouraged by campus administration, students should insist on it.

REFERENCES

1 Irene Kampen, *Due to Lack of Interest Tomorrow Has Been Canceled,* Doubleday, New York, 1969, p. 15.
2 Fred Harvey Harrington, *The Future of Adult Education,* Jossey-Bass, San Francisco, 1977, pp. 32–33.

3 Ibid.
4 Faculty Committee on University Outreach Functions, *University of Wisconsin-Madison and Open Education,* University of Wisconsin, Madison, Wisc., 1975.
5 Alexander M. Mood, *The Future of Higher Education,* McGraw-Hill, New York, 1973, p. 25.
6 Graduate School of Social Sciences and Humanities, *Bulletin of the University of Wisconsin-Madison,* University of Wisconsin, Madison, Wisc., 1975, p. 10.
7 References to consider for more information on how to become assertive include Robert E. Alberti and Michael L. Emmons, *Your Perfect Right,* Impact, San Luis Obispo, Calif., 1974; and Alberti and Emmons, *Stand Up Speak Out Talk Back,* Pocket Books, New York, 1975.
8 Harold Taylor, *How to Change Colleges,* Holt, New York, 1971, p. 62.
9 Mood, op. cit., p. 88.
10 Ibid., p. 107.
11 Paulo Freire, *Pedagogy of the Oppressed,* Herder and Herder, New York, 1970.
12 Chere Sandra Coggins, "Application of the Freire Method in North America: An Exploratory Study with Implications for Adult Education," unpublished master of science thesis, University of Wisconsin, Madison, Wisc., 1973, pp. 47–52.

INDEX